Luigi Giussani

In Search of the Human Face

Translated by
Matthew Henry

With the assistance of
Laura Ferrario & Gregory Wolfe

SLANT
BOOKS

IN SEARCH OF THE HUMAN FACE

Slant Books
P.O. Box 60295
Seattle, WA 98160
www.slantbooks.org

Cataloguing-in-Publication data:

Names: Giussani, Luigi.

Title: In search of the human face / Luigi Giussani.

Description: Seattle, WA: Slant Books, 2025

Identifiers: ISBN 978-1-63982-191-4 (hardcover) | ISBN 978-1-63982-190-7 (paperback) | ISBN 978-1-63982-192-1 (ebook)

Subjects: LCSH: Spirituality | Pastoral theology | Religion and ethics | Christian ethics

Contents

Introduction

THE SUPREME OBSTACLE to our human path is the neglect of the I. Opposition to such neglect, an interest in our own I—here lies the first step on a truly human path.

It would seem obvious for one to have this interest, while it cannot be taken for granted: it suffices to look at the great abyss of emptiness that opens up in our daily life, in our awareness, and in our loss of memory. In fact, the constitutive factors of the human subject are not captured in the abstract; they are not a prejudice but become evident when the I is in action, when the subject is engaged with reality.

Behind the word "I" we see a great confusion today, and yet an understanding of what exactly is *my subject* is of primary importance. Indeed, this subject is at the center, at the root of all my actions (even thinking is an action). Action is the dynamic with which I enter into relationship with each thing, each person. If I neglect my own I, it is impossible for my relationships to be mine, for my life (the sky, a woman, a friend, music) to be mine.

In order to say *my* with seriousness, I need to have a clear perception of what constitutes my own I. Nothing is as fascinating as the discovery of the true dimension of my I, nothing so rich in surprises as the discovery of my own human face.

And nothing is so moving as the fact that God became man to give me a definitive help, to accompany with discretion, with tenderness and power, the arduous journey of each person in search of the human face. God not only shows his fatherhood in the creation of all things and in ruling over their destiny and their circumstances, but also and especially in his drawing-near, as an unlooked-for and unanticipated companion, on the path where every person grows toward his destiny.

The first observation at the beginning of every serious inquiry into the constitution of the subject is that the confusion that dominates today behind the fragile mask (almost a *flatus vocis*) of our I comes in part from external influences on our person. We need to keep in mind the decisive influence of what the Gospel calls "the world," which shows itself as the enemy of a stable, dignified, and consistent formation of the human personality. There is an incredibly strong pressure from the world that surrounds us (through the mass media and even through education and politics), that influences and ends up choking—as a prejudice—any attempt to become aware of our own I. Paradoxically, if we smash our finger on the bus or at school, we are very quick to react, to get angry. If instead it happens—and it does happen—that our I gets smashed, literally suppressed or intimidated into remaining numb to our true personality, this we calmly bear every day.

The success of such an oppression or intimidation is clear: by now the same word "I" evokes something confused and fluctuating for the vast majority of people, a term that we use for convenience, with a purely indicative meaning (like "bottle" or "cup"). But behind that little word, there no longer vibrates anything, anything that can powerfully and clearly indicate the type of understanding and feeling one can have of the value of one's I.

Therefore, we can say that we are living in a time when civilization seems to be ending: the evolution of a civilization, in fact, is revealed in the measure that it fosters the coming to light and the clarification of the value of the individual I. We are in an age when, instead, the culture fosters a great confusion in regard to the content of the word "I."

The inevitable and literally tragic consequence of such a reality, in which the reality of the I is dissolved, is the dissolution of the term "you."

Today we no longer know how to say "you" to anyone. And here is the ultimate and hidden root of the violence and of the quest for power that largely determine normal relationships between people today: these relationships, in fact, are generally based on the systematic reduction of the other to a desire to possess or use, in the absence of any amazement or feeling for the existence of the other.

The confusion that alters the contours of the human face is the apex of a crisis which has very precise historical and existential origins. In the individual experience of a Western person of our time, this confusion is re-lived according to the same steps that have been verified in history: individual experience and historical experience coincide. As we have sketched elsewhere (cf. *Religious Awareness in Modern Man*, 1998), there was an age in which humanity began to make the claim to be the measure—and thus the master—of reality. It had to do with a humanism in which reason—which is the instrument with which the person opens up to reality to the point of its ultimate horizon as mystery—was conceived no longer as openness, but as measure, as the ultimate guarantee of the existence of reality, as the cage into which the inexhaustible nature of reality had to be squeezed. Humanity lifted itself up as the measure of everything, succeeding in reducing everything to the measure of its capacity and its power over these things. It tried to base the dignity and even the value of the human person on the outcome of its attempts at power, on its capacity to dominate reality. In this change, the variety of facts that make up the human personality and the human community ceased to form a unity. The figure of the saint—which indicates the exemplary image of a human personality which lives a non-fragmented experience of the I, of the world, and of history—was replaced by man as "god," stretched forth to impose his lordship over every field, in a reality understood more and more in a fragmentary way. In this fragmentation of experience, God became a useless reality, to the point that, although professed, the relationship with God was understood as a relationship with an abstraction, as an indecisive factor in the determination and concrete development of existence. The presence of God to the conscience of an individual and to his earthly life was felt in a hostile way. Many factors contributed to this passage—cultural, psychological, and ecclesial—which we have examined elsewhere (cf. *Religious Awareness in Modern Man*). In fact, the period that followed the Middle Ages was completely informed by this claim to make God less determinative for the human face and for humanity's relationship with reality.

The exhaustion of this claim coincides with its most extreme form.

In every century, we see the evidence of the incapacity of humanity to recognize its own face and to establish adequate relationships—that is, relationships that are not marked by lies, by censure, or by a possessiveness that only leaves us wounded—with the reality where we live. When God is eliminated as the wellspring and the law of life, reality becomes incomprehensible, elusive, precisely at the point which should be the center of awareness: the I. And so, with such confusion, the only energy that allows the natural propensity of people to come together and communicate seems to be that which is guaranteed by power, in its double modes of conformism and instrumentalization. The tragic feeling of this defeat is witnessed in a moving and clear way in all the greatest artistic and philosophical works of our age: a testimony which displays the tragic sense of life and where there emerges the great longing for meaning and for a presence (for God) whose existence we intuit, but whose face and dwelling remain unknown. "There exists a point of arrival, but no way to reach it," said Kafka, expressing with deep lucidity this strange contradiction: reason, by its very nature, recognizes the existence of a purpose, of truth, but everything seems dark; every bridge that people would throw toward that purpose is destined to fail—there is no way to reach it. Kafka's sentence condemns everyone to despair, but, not allowing for the possible initiatives of that "point of arrival," it shows a disloyalty in the face of reason. Indeed, by doing this, it holds us back from the tension and the expectation in front of the mystery of existence, throwing us instead into a grotesque "unreasonable security"; reason, in fact, if free, continues to attempt to find the "way," leaving open every possibility. The category of "possibility" best defines the dynamic of reason, whatever method reason follows (cf. *Religious Awareness in Modern Man*).

In the confusion surrounding the ultimate face of the I and of reality, an extreme attempt is developing today that would pursue this flight from the relationship with the infinite Mystery which every reasonable man sees as the horizon and root of every human experience: we are told to deny any ultimate consistency in life. If reality seems to escape one's every attempt at mastery, the extreme resource of pride is to deny reality any consistency, arbitrarily considering everything as an illusion or a game. We call "nihilism" that which reigns today in the world of thought and the worldview of the dominant culture. But it is a nihilism that does not even have a tragic feeling for the defeat behind it and rather conceals this tragedy in a false reduction of everything to a game, to an arbitrary invitation to skepticism and moral superficiality.

For two thousand years, the encounter with the Christian event has been the encounter with a human phenomenon (a man, a companionship) in which the passion for the discovery of the human face and the openness to reality are strangely awakened. This passion is continually reawakened by something that is not the result of our thoughts or of a particular philosophy.

The first two who followed Jesus along the banks of the Jordan are the first protagonists, after the Virgin Mary, of the mysterious re-conquest of our humanity: these were the first protagonists of the encounter with Christ, with this exceptional presence in history. In the Gospel, in which, after so many years, John wrote down his memory of that day, of the encounter with Jesus by the Jordan, of having followed him after the strange words of the Baptist who pointed him out, of the visit to the house where after their question he simply responded, "Come and see," all these things are described. And yet, as François Mauriac recognizes in a page of his *Life of Jesus*, this episode remains the most moving episode of the Gospel. In fact, it tells of a precise, historic encounter (it even tells us the time: four in the afternoon!), but in the notes of the disciple almost everything is left implicit. We can imagine what is said only implicitly, seeing how it would become explicit and change the life of those two fishermen, but already their humanity and their heart in that first decisive encounter were struck by a presentiment, by an initial but certain piece of evidence: no man ever spoke like him; they had never met anyone like him. After many years, how many other things they saw and understood, albeit confusedly, about what he started to tell them that day; and still the exceptionality of that encounter remained intact to the eyes of the elderly evangelist. Their heart, that day, ran into a presence that corresponded in an unexpected and clear way to the desire for truth, for beauty, for justice which constituted their simple and humble humanity. From that moment, notwithstanding a thousand betrayals and misunderstandings, they would never abandon him; they became his.

Quickly, that presence impressed on their life an urgency to change, to see their humanity fulfilled, with an urgency so powerful that history would be transformed by their action and holiness would enter this world as an unimagined experience of purity and human fruitfulness. The Christian event, in fact, has the inevitable consequence of inaugurating a new type of morality. This morality flourishes not through submission to rules, which are dictated in the end (even in an alleged "individual" morality) by the common mentality and thus by the power that influences the majority, but rather from the recognition of an exceptional encounter. It is a morality, a change of judgment and action, that happens according to the dynamic put forward by Romano Guardini: "In the experience of a great love, everything that happens becomes an event within its sphere." In fact, the presence of Christ and his friendship introduce a new capacity to look at and treat people and things according to all the factors at play: with a respect and an attention to particulars and to destiny. In this sense, true morality consists, as true reason, in a tension toward a conscious openness to all the factors at play in reality.

At a moment in which the very word "morality" has become nebulous—that is, when it is used instrumentally and hypocritically in the struggle for power—we have the urgent and exciting task of rediscovering what an authentic moral tension consists of and how it is formed.

A man called himself God: a phenomenon began that belongs in a particular way to the sphere of religious experience, that is, to that series of questions and attempts by which people in all times seek to know the meaning of their lives and to establish a connection between the finiteness of their human face and the infinite mystery of their destiny. With Christ, in fact, the method is reversed, that way along which every serious attempt at relationship with the Mystery had walked, where God appeared as the *terra incognita* of the ancient maps. It is no longer the person who seeks to establish a relationship with a distant God, employing in surprising and moving ways their imagination and devotion; it is God who has become a companion to that one in the most concrete and discreet way possible. In the human relationship with this Jesus—who walked, ate, cried, and acted with such goodness and power that, upon seeing these things, one could not help but think of a divine action, for the first twelve and all along the path of history to us—the way to enter into relationship with the Mystery which makes everything is revealed, the way toward understanding our destiny as children and ultimately our own human face. As John Paul II wrote in his first, fundamental encyclical, *Redemptor Hominis*: "Man remains a being that is incomprehensible to himself, his life is senseless if he does not encounter Jesus Christ. This is why Christ the Redeemer fully reveals man to himself." Jesus Christ reveals the road not because he imposes it (and he could have—he is God!), but because he communicates himself through the most fitting and respectful dynamic of human consciousness: he, in fact (as we outlined in *At the Origin of the Christian Claim*), reveals himself as a presence that corresponds in an exceptional way to the most natural desires of the human heart and mind. He shows that exceptionality because he is the man in front of whom the human heart recognizes the correspondence for which it was naturally made and which one never tastes—not even in front of the most important and beautiful experiences of his life—except as a brief moment that ultimately leaves one sad. No one is like him; those who are his own must recognize it. If they did not believe him—as St. Peter says with instinctive clarity—they could not believe their own eyes. This exceptional evidence does not annul but rather exalts human freedom: in front of the "come and follow me" repeated without distinction to fishermen, mafiosi, prostitutes, wise men, and politicians, everyone is called to "reveal the thoughts of their hearts," to decide whether to adhere to the truth more than to their own ideas or advantage.

Christianity, then, has presented itself from its first appearance in the world as an event. It is the birth of a child at Bethlehem; it is, physically and historically, the infancy and youth of Jesus in the sight of the amazed eyes of Mary; it is the encounter with John and Andrew and all the other encounters that have communicated him in every corner of the earth down to our own day.

The category of event is, after all, the most adequate to human consciousness and experience, whether it has to do with knowledge of the I or any other type of knowledge: it is a primary category, because only an event puts in motion and can alter a serious process of knowledge.

The continuity of this exceptional presence in the world and in history is given in the human flow of which Christ is the head: it is his body, the Church. She is the "Stranger," as T.S. Eliot called her, a human reality whose consciousness and existence is determined by a factor that does not belong to the world and to man: the Church, as we have studied in depth (cf. *Why the Church?*, "The Effective Sign of the Divine in History"), is that historical phenomenon in which the divine is communicated through the human, it is the re-happening of the event of Christ. Therefore, in belonging to the experience of the Church, the form of a morality that is specifically Christian finds support and force.

"The true drama of a Church that loves to define itself as modern—John Paul I said—is the attempt to replace the wonder of the event of Christ with rules." Today, while the dramatic question of T.S. Eliot in *Choruses from "The Rock"* resounds ("Has the Church abandoned humanity, or has humanity abandoned the Church?"), the Spirit, who is the energy with which God acts in the world, does not stop raising up men and women with that same amazement that John and Andrew had in front of the Christian event. In far-off places, in the most remote territories, the event of Christ lives again—and even in places where we work and live, which are so often and tragically deserts of humanity. Still, just like and even more than in the epoch of the great Benedictine movement, Christians communicate a positivity of experience to the world, a force of charity serving all people. This happens where Christianity is not reduced to a discourse—to "Word" and to a consequent subjectivism—but exists as an experience of an event in the present. That which does not exist as a present experience does not exist: to be contemporary with Christ is the only condition needed to understand how in him all things hold together (Colossians 1), as the beginning of a new people (Galatians 3), as the criterion with which to face the whole of experience (catholicity), and as the origin of a cultural position, a worldview that allows us to test everything and retain what is good (1 Thessalonians. 5).

So in front of the event of Christ—which is the most extraordinary event in human history and which invests everything with a thrilling value—the question that arises and measures the seriousness and passion with which every person looks at his or her own life is: what is this all about?

Milan, 22 February 1995

PART I

A Dramatic Path

Where Is the Consistency of Man?

God, Man's Destiny

EACH OF US, if we reflect, can observe what are the most habitual factors in our intelligence, in our dreams, in our feelings, that come together to form in us an image of ourselves as a human being.

These factors represent the sense that we have of ourselves and of others, because others resemble us; they will give us the measure of what we consider essential elements of our humanity.

But arriving at an understanding of what constitutes our image of man is not *a* point of some discourse: it is *the* point, where all the energies of our sensibility, our affectivity, and our intelligence converge in expectation of fulfillment.

I will not pause here to describe the various representations of humanity that are typical of our society and our time.

I will just say that for a true person, the Lord is everything. The Lord: that is, the Mystery from which everything flows in its totality in every instant.

The Bible introduces the human like this in its account of creation: "Then God said, 'Let us make humankind in our image, according to our likeness'" (Genesis 1:26).

The biblical story makes us confront immediately the characteristics of a nature whose destiny is God.

Therefore, if the intrinsic destiny of our nature is the Lord, then the Lord is everything. The Bible shows us in quick sequence how the expression "the Lord is everything" is an experience in life: "They heard the sound of the Lord God walking in the garden at the time of the evening breeze"

(Genesis 3:8). The biblical author wants to give the idea of an existential familiarity of God with the person, of the habit of the divine presence that characterized the life of man and woman before sin.

The Lord is everything not because of a feeling, because we *feel* that he is everything; not because of an act of the will, because we *decide* that he is everything; not moralistically, because he *should* be everything, but by nature.

But the fact that the Lord is everything by nature did not emerge as the fruit of wisdom; it did not come out of a philosophical reflection. That the Lord is the Lord because he makes us, and thus determines our life, became evident through his intervention in history, through an historical revelation.

God revealed the person's destiny by revealing himself; he made known the name of human destiny through his presence; he intervened in order to remind us that he is the destiny of each one, the *unum* capable of making our life more human. And history is the long story of the reshaping of human pride, which tends to make its own image of its destiny, which tends to base the constitutive factors of its physiognomy on its total autonomy.

God Reveals Himself as Lord through History

In order to define the person in a concrete way, God manifests himself in relationship with them as *Lord of history*. And the Bible gives us, again, the primordial references to this manifestation, above all in laying out for us the exemplary story of Abraham's vocation:

> Now the Lord said to Abram, "Go from your country and your kindred and your father's house to the land that I will show you. I will make of you a great nation, and I will bless you, and make your name great, so that you will be a blessing. I will bless those who bless you, and the one who curses you I will curse; and in you all the families of the earth shall be blessed." So Abram went, as the Lord had told him. . . (Genesis 12:1-4).

We read here the movement this man's life took upon itself, in the sudden and mysterious manifestation of God, a destiny that was not his, even if it ultimately corresponded to his nature. That departure was the response to a command, the recognition of a clear authority. So this mysterious

God—who showed him the path—was the Lord of his path, of the path of meaning, of human meaning.

What defined Abraham's sense of self was that voice—or that presence—that said to him: "Go from your country and your kindred and your father's house to the land that I will show you." The image we are trying to invoke is that of a man in whose eyes, in the content of whose thoughts, in the way he confronted problems, anxieties, aspirations, and fears, kept that presence alive.

This is evident also in Genesis 15, the chapter of the covenant: God becomes event; he engages intimately the life of that man, putting himself alongside Abraham.

> After these things the word of the Lord came to Abram in a vision, "Do not be afraid, Abram, I am your shield; your reward shall be very great." But Abram said, "O Lord God, what will you give me, for I continue childless, and the heir of my house is Eliezer of Damascus?" And Abram said, "You have given me no offspring, and so a slave born in my house is to be my heir." But the word of the Lord came to him, "This man shall not be your heir; no one but your very own issue shall be your heir." He brought him outside and said, "Look toward heaven and count the stars, if you are able to count them." Then he said to him, "So shall your descendants be." And he believed the Lord; and the Lord reckoned it to him as righteousness (Genesis 15:1-6).

Here it jumps out how the most realistic project in the life of Abraham is not his, but the project of another. And this project, if we accept it in its initial manifestation, can be verified in time. Thus, Abraham will prove his familiarity with that presence, which had first overwhelmed him and pulled him far away from home, in the episode by the terebinth of Mamre (Genesis 18) in which the mysterious being will be a guest to serve and feed, under the shade of the tree "in the hottest part of the day."

That presence becomes an ineffable reality of table fellowship. The three guests speak as if they are only one person; from the enigmatic and mysterious fascination of their relationship with Abraham, they turn their gaze to Sarah, Abraham's wife, who has still not borne children: "Next year you will have a child"—and Sarah laughs. And they reprove Abraham for Sarah's laughter, and when Sarah tries to deny it, they say: "No, you did laugh." Can we imagine Abraham thinking of himself without also perceiving that presence? No, in that relationship was the sustenance of his life as well as the expression of that life. Thus, as the ultimate test of that relationship, of that path walked together, of that familiar involvement with God, he will ask Abraham to offer his son:

> So Abraham rose early in the morning, saddled his donkey, and took two of his young men with him, and his son Isaac; he cut the wood for the burnt offering, and set out and went to the place in the distance that God had shown him (Genesis 22:3).

Only an effort of identification can bring us closer to such humanity: let us try to penetrate the soul of that man who gets up to go and sacrifice his son, his only son, and who did not know where, because the Lord would show him where. How attuned must his consciousness have been to adhere to what was asked of him, because his consciousness was woven together with that presence: Abraham would not be Abraham if he had refused. This is why he became the prototype of all those whom the Lord would one day choose.

That the Lord is the Lord, the meaning of life, appears as an observation of experience that is realized in history, in the course of a daily familiarity, like a spark but also like an authentic call, of that first familiarity with the divine that we see in the first chapters of Genesis.

The Person Identified by Relationship with God

Another important reference to the human image, which God wanted to manifest by intervening in history to reveal himself, is found in the figure of Moses. This fundamental fact for the life of a person is re-proposed in the life of Moses: God, from whom everything comes, would remain something vague and would not determine our life if he did not enter life as a factor in it, a determining factor which gives life significance, density, value.

We see it in the third and fourth chapters of Exodus, where a great difference with respect to his earlier existence enters into the life of Moses, where it becomes clear that the Lord is "the Lord" in his life, because he has an encounter that chooses him *for*, that designates him to fulfill a task full of significance and historical effect. This encounter gives Moses a law for his life: it forms him, it gives him a face, it makes his person something that is handed down to us: significant for humanity.

> Moses was keeping the flock of his father-in-law Jethro, the priest of Midian; he led his flock beyond the wilderness, and came to Horeb, the mountain of God. There the angel of the Lord

> appeared to him in a flame of fire out of a bush; he looked, and the bush was blazing, yet it was not consumed. Then Moses said, "I must turn aside and look at this great sight, and see why the bush is not burned up." When the Lord saw that he had turned aside to see, God called to him out of the bush, "Moses, Moses!" And he said, "Here I am." Then he said, "Come no closer! Remove the sandals from your feet, for the place on which you are standing is holy ground." He said further, "I am the God of your father, the God of Abraham, the God of Isaac, and the God of Jacob." And Moses hid his face, for he was afraid to look at God.
>
> Then the Lord said, "I have observed the misery of my people who are in Egypt; I have heard their cry on account of their taskmasters. Indeed, I know their sufferings, and I have come down to deliver them from the Egyptians, and to bring them up out of that land to a good and broad land, a land flowing with milk and honey, to the country of the Canaanites, the Hittites, the Amorites, the Perizzites, the Hivites, and the Jebusites. The cry of the Israelites has now come to me; I have also seen how the Egyptians oppress them. So come, I will send you to Pharaoh to bring my people, the Israelites, out of Egypt." But Moses said to God, "Who am I that I should go to Pharaoh, and bring the Israelites out of Egypt?" He said, "I will be with you; and this shall be the sign for you that it is I who sent you: when you have brought the people out of Egypt, you shall worship God on this mountain" (Exodus 3:1-12).

And we also get to observe Moses's resistance in front of the task for which he was chosen, through his objections and the emphatic response on the part of the Lord.

"Then Moses answered, 'But suppose they do not believe me or listen to me, but say, "The Lord did not appear to you"'" (Exodus 4:1). God will show Moses signs of his absolute dominion over nature, will show him that through men the Egyptians will see wonders. But not even the wonders convince Moses: he objects that he is not very eloquent.

> Then the Lord said to him, "Who gives speech to mortals? Who makes them mute or deaf, seeing or blind? Is it not I, the Lord? Now go, and I will be with your mouth and teach you what you are to speak" (Exodus 4:11-12).

Moses will refuse, and God will be irritated. He promises Moses the help of Aaron and his continual presence, until the man, now defeated, accepts what it means to be a man, that is, one who belongs to God, efficacious and true according to the measure of God's design.

From that moment, that voice that came out of the burning bush and all that great, dramatic, mysterious familiarity totally dominated and determined Moses. If someone came to him and asked: "But who are you, what are you doing?" we can only imagine his response, but he would certainly have attempted a definition that affirmed a consistency in himself. He would maybe have said something like "I am in the hand of God," or "I am this presence."

Instead, for us, in practice, in the course of our existence, an image of a person constituted by the presence of another, by the companionship of another, by the lordship of another, is like a fairy tale. When we get up in the morning, when we have difficulties or disappointments, anxieties or mishaps, the image of another who accompanies and guides us, who comes down to restore us to ourselves, is like a dream. And yet a mother who takes her child by the hand is not a fairy tale: it is the transmission of life. We should at least have the sincerity to put ourselves always in front of this alternative: the presence and the companionship of God is either a fairy tale or the truth of our life, the truth of our humanity.

The Lord, a Companionship that Marks the Life of a People

A last series of biblical references completes this reflection on the revelation of the image of the person through the manifestation of God.

It has to do with the story of a people: God revealed himself within that story, as the companion who determined the meaning of their path. He was truly the Lord of life, of life in so far as it is a reality that moves toward a goal, that is, as history. He was truly the Lord of history. This famous line from Deuteronomy expresses it for us:

> Hear, O Israel: The Lord is our God, the Lord alone. You shall love the Lord your God with all your heart, and with all your soul, and with all your might. Keep these words that I am commanding you today in your heart. Recite them to your children and talk about them when you are at home and when you are away, when you lie down and when you rise. Bind them as a sign on your hand, fix them as an emblem on your forehead, and write them on the doorposts of your house and on your gates (Deuteronomy 6:4-9).

And verse 15 of the same chapter will say: "The Lord your God . . . is present with you." The idea of an a-historical, transcendent God is not practicable as the object of a living knowledge for man. The "God is present with you" is, we can say, a necessity for one who wants to live the organic link with their origin and destiny. The short prayer of Moses in the thirty-third chapter of Exodus expresses this, when he says to the Lord:

> Now if I have found favor in your sight, show me your ways, so that I may know you and find favor in your sight. Consider too that this nation is your people." He said, "My presence will go with you, and I will give you rest." And he said to him, "If your presence will not go, do not carry us up from here. For how shall it be known that I have found favor in your sight, I and your people, unless you go with us? In this way, we shall be distinct, I and your people, from every people on the face of the earth."
>
> The Lord said to Moses, "I will do the very thing that you have asked; for you have found favor in my sight, and I know you by name." Moses said, "Show me your glory, I pray." And he said, "I will make all my goodness pass before you, and will proclaim before you the name, 'The Lord'; and I will be gracious to whom I will be gracious, and will show mercy on whom I will show mercy (Exodus 33:13-19).

One would like to contemplate the glory of God as if in a moment outside time, but God reiterates his inaccessibility—he will say in fact soon after this passage: "You have not seen my face"—but at the same time, his desire to be in relationship with his creature, a relationship whose dynamic comes through his intervention. In the biblical text, he will repeatedly call himself a jealous God, capable of wrath, who will "wipe you from the face of the earth" if you abandon him.

The choice between this jealous God, who is in the midst of the people, and something "other" which can attract one, is a radical choice: between life and death. A person has two ways in front of him: one way which distances oneself from their true nature, to the point of death; with the other following Another from whom this true nature would spring and be sure.

> Surely, this commandment that I am commanding you today is not too hard for you, nor is it too far away. It is not in heaven, that you should say, "Who will go up to heaven for us, and get it for us so that we may hear it and observe it?" Neither is it beyond the sea, that you should say, "Who will cross to the other side of the sea for us, and get it for us so that we may hear it and observe it?" No, the word is very near to you; it is in your mouth and in your heart for you to observe.

> See, I have set before you today life and prosperity, death and adversity. If you obey the commandments of the Lord your God that I am commanding you today, by loving the Lord your God, walking in his ways, and observing his commandments, decrees, and ordinances, then you shall live and become numerous, and the Lord your God will bless you in the land that you are entering to possess. But if your heart turns away and you do not hear, but are led astray to bow down to other gods and serve them, I declare to you today that you shall perish; you shall not live long in the land that you are crossing the Jordan to enter and possess. I call heaven and earth to witness against you today that I have set before you life and death, blessings and curses. Choose life so that you and your descendants may live, loving the Lord your God, obeying him, and holding fast to him; for that means life to you and length of days, so that you may live in the land that the Lord swore to give to your ancestors, to Abraham, to Isaac, and to Jacob (Deuteronomy 30:11-20).

The Method of Revelation

All these emblematic references to God's manifestation have something in common, something that characterizes the action of the Lord. That God manifests himself as Lord of history by intervening in history means that he has to use the *particular*, because history is made up of particulars, and that means that God *chooses* this particular. Precisely this chosen particular, this particular with which he identifies himself in a gesture of love, demonstrates to everyone who God is, the Lord of humanity.

> It was not because you were more numerous than any other people that the Lord set his heart on you and chose you—for you were the fewest of all peoples. It was because the Lord loved you and kept the oath that he swore to your ancestors, that the Lord has brought you out with a mighty hand, and redeemed you from the house of slavery, from the hand of Pharaoh king of Egypt. Know therefore that the Lord your God is God, the faithful God who maintains covenant loyalty with those who love him and keep his commandments, to a thousand generations (Deuteronomy 7:7-9).

If we allow ourselves to pause in front of the categories that emerge in this revelation of the Lord, we should grasp, at least in a fleeting way, how huge is the distance between it and the categories that rule our usual ideas, our feelings, our expectations. The Lord did not appear on the horizon of human thought and human inquiry as something confused, partial, fragmented; instead, through the choice of a particular—becoming a factor in a particular history, entering the history of a particular people—God comes into the story of everyone as the only Lord: "The Lord is one."

God is not a mysteriousness that surrounds us nebulously from afar, who intervenes from outside like a suffocating restriction, like bars of laws, a prison in which we are caged: he emerges from within, a spring, a deep companionship without whom we can do nothing. He emerges from within our existence, because he constitutes us and wants to be brought into the things of which life is made, because otherwise we would not live. We need to discover and follow him within the reality of existence, because he is the God of the living, and the realities of existence would be mere appearances, schematic and formal, without him.

In this way, we are called to experience the meaning of our humanity through the mode of his revelation, the way his presence within historical existence is recorded and produced.

Resistance to the Truth About Ourselves

The Illusion of Autonomy

ONE ACTS IN one's own life and in history, but what meaning—origin, structure, and aim—does that action have? God. Outside of this word, there is nothing. The adequate criterion for one's action is God, to live one's life in the sight of God.

Instead, from the beginning, one tries to divest oneself of the image of a creature who is made "in the likeness" of God, tends to set up life according to one's measure, which in a more or less complex way is nothing other than the reactivity of the moment, whether it presents itself as a state of the soul, as instinct, or as opinion. It is the attempt to make the moment infinite and claim an eternal value for it, whereas, in reality, things are the other way around: only the infinite can give eternal value to the moment. The goal of our actions always cries out for infinity, like the voice of one who desires the indelible outline of a face that should be his.

Ramuz, a Swiss writer, says: "One can love what does not endure only in the name of something that does endure." But the survival of an authentic cry does not prevent the fact that the reactivity of the moment becomes our dominant mentality, becomes theorized, defended, becomes a general lie.

This general lie at the level of awareness is also a temptation for the little people whom God has chosen, but is manifested in a more dramatic way as a struggle between the *self* and a mysterious measure: it is as if one must walk, giving oneself completely to something that does not correspond to any human measure, and find joy after one has abandoned oneself to it; but typically there is difficulty, resistance, and rebellion.

There is a beautiful verse from the prophet Jeremiah that I want to recall because it powerfully expresses this dialectic in the relationship between God and his people, between God and the person.

> Thus says the Lord:
> I remember the devotion of your youth,
> your love as a bride,
> how you followed me in the wilderness,
> in a land not sown. Israel was holy to the Lord,
> the first fruits of his harvest.
> All who ate of it were held guilty;
> disaster came upon them,
> says the Lord.
> Hear the word of the Lord, O house of Jacob, and all the families of the house of Israel. Thus says the Lord:
> What wrong did your ancestors find in me
> that they went far from me,
> and went after worthless things, and became worthless themselves? (Jeremiah 2:2-5).

Forgetfulness

The verse that recalls "the devotion of your youth," in which God reminds Israel of "how you followed me," leads us to the level of a choice that makes it clear that God is everything, is determinative, that he is Lord of the totality.

This verse from Jeremiah recalls another, more dramatic verse from Ezekiel, in which the trajectory of God's possession of us and our response is depicted in a raw and passionate way. God speaks to his people:

> As for your birth, on the day you were born your navel cord was not cut, nor were you washed with water to cleanse you, nor rubbed with salt, nor wrapped in cloths. No eye pitied you, to do any of these things for you out of compassion for you; but you were thrown out in the open field, for you were abhorred on the day you were born.
>
> I passed by you, and saw you flailing about in your blood. As you lay in your blood, I said to you, "Live! and grow up like a plant of the field." You grew up and became tall and arrived at full

> womanhood; your breasts were formed, and your hair had grown; yet you were naked and bare.
>
> I passed by you again and looked on you; you were at the age for love. I spread the edge of my cloak over you, and covered your nakedness: I pledged myself to you and entered into a covenant with you, says the Lord God, and you became mine. Then I bathed you with water and washed off the blood from you, and anointed you with oil. I clothed you with embroidered cloth and with sandals of fine leather; I bound you in fine linen and covered you with rich fabric. I adorned you with ornaments: I put bracelets on your arms, a chain on your neck, a ring on your nose, earrings in your ears, and a beautiful crown upon your head. You were adorned with gold and silver, while your clothing was of fine linen, rich fabric, and embroidered cloth. You had choice flour and honey and oil for food. You grew exceedingly beautiful, fit to be a queen. Your fame spread among the nations on account of your beauty, for it was perfect because of my splendor that I had bestowed on you, says the Lord God.
>
> But you trusted in your beauty, and played the whore because of your fame, and lavished your whorings on any passer-by (Ezekiel 16:3-15).

It is clear here that the position is one of rebellion for the sake of affirming one's reactivity, one's instinctiveness: in the powerful figure of this woman who throws it all away in the fickleness of her feelings. Jeremiah will say the same in other words: "You have done all the evil that you could" (Jeremiah 3:5).

Indeed, the person is that level of nature that seeks meaning; otherwise one could not live, one would die: the evil of life—the absence of meaning—kills. So a person seeks meaning either in a self-justifying pride, as in ideology, or in "letting oneself go" in pleasure and satisfaction. But all this is literally "nothing," as the verse from the second chapter of Jeremiah which we mentioned reminds us: God asks himself what injustice his people have found in him that they have decided to follow after nothing and therefore have decided to become nothing. And the same section continues describing in an amazing way this vacuity, this emptiness. Let us see where this emptiness resides: the people do not ask where the Lord is who brought them out of Egypt, who freed them and led them through the desert to a land they could inhabit. They did not ask this question. And it is the question we also forget to ask. Where is the Lord who brought us out of nothing, not so that we would return to nothing, but so that we would live? Where is the Lord from whom we have learned every value of life and culture and the heart of our culture, of our civilization?

Such forgetfulness defines the emptiness of humanity.

Corruption

Only abuse and irrationality can be born from this. Thus the paradigmatic passage from the prophet Jeremiah continues: "when you entered you defiled my land" (Jeremiah 2:7). And then the unreasonable: "they have forsaken me, the fountain of living water" (Jeremiah 2:13).

This is the disappearance of good sense and human intelligence, the disappearance of the human being.

And then Israel, in front of these accusations from God, that the passage from Jeremiah retraces for us, on the one hand denies: "I am not defiled" (Jeremiah 2:23), and on the other hand contradicts itself, raising up her challenge: "It is hopeless, for I have loved strangers, and after them I will go" (Jeremiah 2:25). In spite of this, they maintain their presumption toward God:

> They say to a tree, "You are my father,"
> and to a stone, "You gave me birth."
> For they have turned their backs to me,
> and not their faces.
> But in the time of their trouble they say,
> "Come and save us!" (Jeremiah 2:27).

This dialectic between the offer of solidity and the stubborn pursuit of the void, between the unavoidable recognition of infidelity and their vain justifications, ends up with the declaration that God has to make, that puts us to shame:

> You say, "I am innocent;
> surely his anger has turned from me."
> Now I am bringing you to judgment
> for saying, "I have not sinned."
> How lightly you gad about,
> changing your ways! (Jeremiah 2:35-36).

Alienation

In this position, one destroys oneself, consumes oneself. The things in which they trusted will devour them. Time becomes the enemy of the human, because the more time goes on, the more it burns one up: in fact, everything shows its unreality, its vanity. And the more one multiplies relationships that become everything, the more one is devoured, becomes an instrument of others, becomes alienated.

Either we adhere with our whole being to the living God of history, within that story where he has revealed himself and revealed us to ourselves, or we are the instrument of others, the instrument of those who are temporarily stronger. Because time makes us always more erratic and fragile, always more invested and invaded by a dominant mentality.

So, becoming aware of this resistance to the truth about ourselves as human beings, having a sense of sin, is the most pedagogically important thing in life, because it opens us to the true God. To sin is to behave like we are the masters of our own life, and to recognize sin is to come closer to the fact that the measure, the criterion, the lordship of our life is the mystery of God.

So the truth about man has a double source: God is everything, and we do not recognize it. We can accomplish something good for ourselves only starting from this truth.

Through the Refusal of Man, the Mercy of God

Only because God, in electing a people, inserts himself into our physical path as a fact of experience, identifies himself with a time and a place, becomes a companion who existentially determines life—only for this reason can we feel that God "presses near" in a way that cannot be diluted or interpreted away. And only then does our reaction take flesh, within our own existence and movement in time and space, because everything in us is linked miserably to our reaction, but that presence contradicts it.

And the flesh of our existence means the people to whom we belong, with its leaders and prophets, its events and relationships and laws.

The irresistible contagion of Adam's sin, in those who live life following themselves and what they want (while they are made by God and find their meaning in God), reveals itself in the historical event of Israel, a historical event in which God is involved.

Without the election—without God who becomes history—one's true stature would not be revealed; this Adam who was made for a total meaning and who tries to identify his destiny, the significance of his gestures, with his reaction: what vanity! Thus the one who is made for life must die! Through a history, God reveals this profound division in us, between what one is—infinite thirst—and one's existence which moves in contradiction, because the norm is not the mystery, but one's own vanity.

Even this division teaches us to understand who God is for us, to glimpse the nature of his life.

Who God is for us, what we are called to understand, our meaning and destiny, is compassion, mercy. We cannot understand this word well, when it shows itself definitively in history, if we do not walk the great path of prophecy in Israel.

> For the Lord has called you
> like a wife forsaken and grieved in spirit,
> like the wife of a man's youth when she is cast off,
> says your God.
> For a brief moment I abandoned you,
> but with great compassion I will gather you.
> In overflowing wrath for a moment
> I hid my face from you,
> but with everlasting love I will have compassion on you (Isaiah 54:6-8).

All the prophets are called to remind Israel of her infidelity toward God, who loved his people with the love of a husband for his wife, but they also have the task of announcing the moving openness of the Lord toward this unfaithful creature:

> And I will take you for my wife forever; I will take you for my wife in righteousness and in justice, in steadfast love, and in mercy. I will take you for my wife in faithfulness; and you shall know the Lord (Hosea 2:19-20).

> When Israel was a child, I loved him,
> and out of Egypt I called my son.
> The more I called them,
> the more they went from me [...]
> I led them with cords of human kindness,
> with bands of love.
> I was to them like those
> who lift infants to their cheeks.

I bent down to them and fed them.[...]
My heart recoils within me;
my compassion grows warm and tender.
I will not execute my fierce anger;
I will not again destroy Ephraim;
for I am God and no mortal (Hosea 11:1-2, 4, 8-9).

The height of God's word about himself is in this supreme word: *mercy*, as if God were saying: "although you are like this, I love you; you rebel against me, and I love you."

The incommensurability of God is clear in this; he is radically different from us:

For my thoughts are not your thoughts,
nor are your ways my ways, says the Lord.
For as the heavens are higher than the earth,
so are my ways higher than your ways
and my thoughts than your thoughts (Isaiah 55:8-9).

The sense of mystery, of the infinite—a vague feeling—becomes a *difference* of behavior in human life.

> Yes, thus says the Lord God: I will deal with you as you have done, you who have despised the oath, breaking the covenant; yet I will remember my covenant with you in the days of your youth, and I will establish with you an everlasting covenant. Then you will remember your ways, and be ashamed when I take your sisters, both your elder and your younger, and give them to you as daughters, but not on account of my covenant with you. I will establish my covenant with you, and you shall know that I am the Lord, in order that you may remember and be confounded, and never open your mouth again because of your shame, when I forgive you all that you have done, says the Lord God (Ezekiel 16:59-63).

And the Bible leaves no doubt about the fact that this difference has to do with the nature of God. The prophet Ezekiel says:

> Thus says the Lord God: It is not for your sake, O house of Israel, that I am about to act, but for the sake of my holy name, which you have profaned among the nations to which you came (Ezekiel 36:22).

And because it is his nature, how can he not leave behind the imprint of his blessing?

Rend your hearts and not your clothing.
Return to the Lord, your God,
for he is gracious and merciful,
slow to anger, and abounding in steadfast love,
and relents from punishing.
Who knows whether he will not turn and relent,
and leave a blessing behind him (Joel 2:13-14).

Mercy and change

We are drawing closer to the point in which we begin to understand, almost seeing with our own eyes, what the mercy of God is and the change it creates in the present. To perceive this mercy means to change. Mercy is a *fact* at work.

The Lord passed before him, and proclaimed,
"The Lord, the Lord,
a God merciful and gracious,
slow to anger,
and abounding in steadfast love and faithfulness,
keeping steadfast love for the thousandth generation,
forgiving iniquity and transgression and sin,
yet by no means clearing the guilty,
but visiting the iniquity of the parents
upon the children
and the children's children,
to the third and the fourth generation" (Exodus 34:6-7).

To perceive the mercy of God means also to perceive the reality of punishment. And this is not a contradiction. The word punishment, in fact, is our way of speaking about how the presence of someone inflicts a penalty. This is a law of reality, in the sense that if one does not use people, things, and above all oneself according to our nature, the deterioration of life is inevitable.

Mercy is something that goes *beyond* the data in our possession—goodness or punishment—and appears contradictory to us. Mercy is not exhausted in the image of the Lord's goodness, and the one who understands this lays the basis for a different effect than the one who looks at goodness and punishment for sin as two separate things. In this different effect, it becomes clear how the concept of punishment deepens that of mercy. If punishment were the only outcome of sin, sin would define us. Instead, despite everything, sin does not define us. In the story of salvation, of the God who progressively reveals the road for rediscovering one's true image, sin is not the last word. And here is the miracle of mercy in Mercy, that is in Being. And so in Mercy, in Being understood as pity, how is one situated? In what way can we live, with all our sin?

If we recognize mercy, we accept ourselves and challenge ourselves to be changed by another, by a merciful other. And this brings about a pain, a true pain, but one that is full of joy. Humanity is happy because God lives. Mercy is a pain that laughs: as happens with children, when they fall down and hurt themselves and their face is covered in tears, but then they smile because mom and dad are with them to console them, to help them.

And so here is the miracle of mercy: the *desire* to change. This defines the new *present* for sinful humanity. The word "present" is essential in this conversation: in fact, when change is left up to our decision—"I should change"—it is always put off to the future, destined to be the fruit of self-love; one would distance oneself from the principal instrument of God: the present.

Thus, we have to be people who are in front of him, begging to be changed, where this asking and this decision are an expression *of ourselves now*. Human beings are fragile and always fall; the question then becomes that of the fundamental structure of our relationship with God—prayer. "In the time of mercy, I heard you," says God in the Old Testament: begging is a decision in the present, but it is also the certainty—if he has revealed himself as mercy—that it will be heard. So, to beg also means to respond, a responsibility toward the concreteness with which that merciful presence has placed himself in the history of each and of all. We start to be true when we recognize our misery, as beggars whose richness comes from asking and depending.

The Image Fulfilled

Imitating God

THIS *BEGGING* which is the truth of our present life—what does it produce? What happens when God hears it? On God's part, helping us and hearing us means involving himself with us, with his power, and therefore making us participate in the destiny which he is. And on our part, the desire for God to change us will mean that we no longer pin our hopes on ourselves but recognize that what we are is him, following the image of the original man: "Let us make man in our image."

If we are in his image, our desire and our begging are the beginning of *imitating him*, the tension of turning our reality into his, of involving ourselves in that structure and that dynamic where he is. Biblical morality is not born from precepts; it is an existential, not a philosophical, morality, deduced from the nature of the person. "You must diligently keep the commandments of the Lord your God, and his decrees, and his statutes that he has commanded you" (Deuteronomy 6:17).

The precepts, though, that God gives us to follow are *manifestations* of his own nature. The God of the Bible is a model to imitate, a historical model, revealed in history.

> When your children ask you in time to come, "What is the meaning of the decrees and the statutes and the ordinances that the Lord our God has commanded you?" then you shall say to your children, "We were Pharaoh's slaves in Egypt, but the Lord brought us out of Egypt with a mighty hand. The Lord displayed before our eyes great and awesome signs and wonders against Egypt, against Pharaoh and all his household. He brought us out from there in order to bring us in, to give us the land that he promised on oath to

> our ancestors. Then the Lord commanded us to observe all these statutes, to fear the Lord our God, for our lasting good, so as to keep us alive, as is now the case. If we diligently observe this entire commandment before the Lord our God, as he has commanded us, we will be in the right" (Deuteronomy 6:20-25).

And what are we to imitate about this God who wanted to manifest himself in the history of a people? The Bible often describes the *goodness* and the *mercy* of the God of Israel, and how this is unique in the panorama of the other divinities worshiped by other peoples. Here is how his *justice* is described:

> Thus says the Lord:
> For three transgressions of Israel,
> and for four, I will not revoke the punishment;
> because they sell the righteous for silver,
> and the needy for a pair of sandals—
> they who trample the head of the poor into the dust of the earth,
> and push the afflicted out of the way;
> father and son go in to the same girl,
> so that my holy name is profaned;
> they lay themselves down beside every altar
> on garments taken in pledge;
> and in the house of their God they drink
> wine bought with fines they imposed.
> Yet I destroyed the Amorite before them,
> whose height was like the height of cedars,
> and who was as strong as oaks;
> I destroyed his fruit above,
> and his roots beneath.
> Also I brought you up out of the land of Egypt,
> and led you forty years in the wilderness,
> to possess the land of the Amorite.
> And I raised up some of your children to be prophets
> and some of your youths to be nazirites.
> Is it not indeed so, O people of Israel?
> says the Lord.
> But you made the nazirites drink wine,
> and commanded the prophets,
> saying, "You shall not prophesy" (Amos 2:6-12).
> I led them with cords of human kindness,
> with bands of love.
> I was to them like those

who lift infants to their cheeks.
I bent down to them and fed them (Hosea 11:4).

My people are bent on turning away from me.
To the Most High they call,
but he does not raise them up at all.
How can I give you up, Ephraim?
How can I hand you over, O Israel?
How can I make you like Admah?
How can I treat you like Zeboiim?
My heart recoils within me;
my compassion grows warm and tender (Hosea 11:7-8).

Who is a God like you, pardoning iniquity
and passing over the transgression
of the remnant of your possession?
He does not retain his anger forever,
because he delights in showing clemency (Micah 7:18).

He has told you, O mortal, what is good;
and what does the Lord require of you
but to do justice, and to love kindness,
and to walk humbly with your God? (Micah 6:8).

Here is a synthesis of all the precepts: to live our devotion as a tension in the sight of God, echoing his features. The culmination of justice, of the imitation of God, is mercy. But we are so far from understanding him that pity and mercy are seen as one *element*, perceived moralistically, a mechanism to respect in certain moments. Yet mercy can be learned, and it is the only possible way of imitating God. In fact, we cannot hope to imitate God in his *creative* capacity, in giving consistency to things, yet we can imitate God's *attitude* toward his creature, toward existence. This is what was true for the prophets of the Old Testament, even if they saw it only from afar: "to walk humbly with your God."

Following Christ

But for twelve Hebrews who lived in Palestine during the Roman Empire, a man in their midst lived the attitude of God.

God made his face visible through a story; but the culmination, the totality of his true revelation to humanity, happened when he became man, entering in person into the story: Jesus Christ. So now the face of human destiny, the nature of the meaning of our existence, is Christ, Christ who is the face of the Father. Christ is the total definition of meaning for human beings in the world.

"For God so loved the world that he gave his only Son, so that everyone who believes in him may not perish but may have eternal life" (John 3:16). Thus, the significance of this Son, of this Word made flesh, is to reveal the fullness of the love of God.

"God's love was revealed among us in this way: God sent his only Son into the world so that we might live through him. In this is love, not that we loved God but that he loved us and sent his Son to be the atoning sacrifice for our sins" (1 John 4:9-10). Christ is our destiny, now made present and accompanying us; the Word made flesh is God's definitive way of being with us, the definitive covenant which he began with his people Israel.

Paradigmatic Encounters

Let us ask ourselves: How was God in this Man? We must look for answers in the Gospel, in some of the encounters that are described there. The first example happens in Matthew, when Jesus accepts an invitation to eat and the others say: "Why do you eat with sinners?" He responds that the sick need a doctor and not the healthy, and that he has not come for the just but for sinners. In the encounter with the sinful woman, who bursts into the middle of a meal and throws herself at his feet, and the host thinks: "This man doesn't know what kind of woman this is," Jesus explains that, "her many sins are forgiven her, because she showed much love." In the episode with Zacchaeus, the rich tax collector, a profession considered the most sinful, whom Jesus surprises up in the tree where Zacchaeus had climbed to see Jesus: "I will come to your house." Again everyone thought: "Who are these people he eats with!" Then Jesus, when Zacchaeus tells him that he will give half of his goods to the poor, reminds everyone: "The Son of Man came to seek and to save what was lost." In the encounter with the woman caught in adultery, whom the Pharisees bring out to condemn, Jesus, after everyone has left, says to her: "No one condemns you? Neither do I condemn you: go, and sin no more."

Moving from one to another of these encounters, and of so many others that we could recount, something like another world emerges from the person of Christ—something, though, which is in "this" world, another way of seeing things compared with the usual laws and conventions. There emerges an image of humanity, which has remained throughout the centuries even for those who do not have faith. It is the true image of humanity: God, that is, mercy. And for the first time in the world's history, God's nature is defined: God is love, love is the very nature of God. "Whoever does not love does not know God, for God is love" (1 John 4:8).

"So we have known and believe the love that God has for us. God is love, and those who abide in love abide in God, and God abides in them" (1 John 4:16).

This is how St. Paul concludes his second letter to the Corinthians: "Finally, brothers and sisters, farewell. Put things in order, listen to my appeal, agree with one another, live in peace; and the God of love and peace will be with you" (2 Corinthians 13:11). God is thus the God of fraternal love and of peace: and the word love, when translated for the sinful, who have to live next to other sinners, is translated as *mercy* and becomes existential only in the experience of forgiveness and compassion. In St. Paul, love as God's very nature operates as an energy that emanates from God (Spirit) and arrives to us through Jesus. It reconciles us to God and reawakens new feelings toward others. "Anyone who does not have the Spirit of Christ does not belong to him. But if Christ is in you, though the body is dead because of sin, the Spirit is life because of righteousness. If the Spirit of him who raised Jesus from the dead dwells in you, he who raised Christ from the dead will give life to your mortal bodies also through his Spirit that dwells in you" (Romans 8:9-11).

Characteristics of the Love That Has Been Revealed

The characteristics of the love that has been revealed in Christ can be summed up in three ways.

The first is the agape of the cross. The historical proof that Christ reveals that love is the face of the Father is his death on a cross, not only as mortification but as love.

"For while we were still weak, at the right time Christ died for the ungodly. Indeed, rarely will anyone die for a righteous person—though perhaps for a good person someone might actually dare to die. But God proves his love for us in that while we still were sinners Christ died for us" (Romans 5:6-8).

"We know love by this, that he laid down his life for us—and we ought to lay down our lives for one another" (1 John 3:16).

The second characteristic consists in the fact that this love is for *everyone.* This is quite different from the attitude that man can reach on his own: "*apud ipsos fides obstinata misericordia in promptu, sed adversos alios hostile odium*" (Tacitus); "Toward your brothers an immediate and fierce sharing; but towards others, a hostile hatred."

The Gospels, on the other hand, often underline the universal horizon of love revealed by God in Christ. "The Son of Man came not to be served but to serve, and to give his life as a ransom for many" (Matthew 20:28). And again: "For this is my blood of the covenant, which is poured out for many for the forgiveness of sins" (Matthew 26:28).

This horizon of love seems to be particularly open to *those who are far away*, the disinherited, physically and morally. "For I have come to call not the righteous but sinners" (Matthew 9:13). "For the Son of Man came to seek out and to save the lost" (Luke 19:10).

And the imitation of God revealed in Christ (the religious imperative) breaks the mold of human love.

Three parables are significant in this regard: the Samaritan (Luke 10:25-27), the Prodigal Son (Luke 15:11-32), and the workers at the eleventh hour (Matthew 20:1-16).

In the first passage, Jesus responds to a doctor of the law who asked him—and the evangelist Luke observes, in order "to put him to the test"—"Who is my neighbor?" The response from Jesus is a brief and effective parable. Jesus concludes by drawing the answer from the one questioning Him: "Which of these three, do you think, was a neighbor to the man who fell into the hands of the robbers?" And the doctor of the law is forced to respond in truth: "The one who showed him mercy." The one who had compassion on the man in difficulty was one considered an enemy of the Jews of that time. So the last indication of Jesus to the doctor of the law is particularly powerful: "Go and do likewise."

Also in the second parable, the bounds of human love are enlarged beyond measure. The father, whose son forgot him but then sought him out in the moment of solitude and desperation, is the great paternal figure of the New Testament. He seems to have been waiting for a long time for the son who ran away from him. Luke notes: "But while he was still far off, his father saw him," and had seemed to be waiting for his son with a love that went beyond any other consideration. The text goes on: and he "was filled with compassion; he ran and put his arms around him and kissed him." Then, the story continues with a feast for the son "who was lost but now is found"; but then a new element is added, with a response that is even more upsetting for our human measure: the jealousy and anger of the older son, the faithful worker, in front of so much joy over a senseless brother. "His father came out and began to plead with him," because the older son did not want to go into the feast. And after the father heard his complaints, he responds to his son, expressing the great criterion of divine love: "Son, you are always with me, and all that is mine is yours. But we had to celebrate and rejoice, because this brother of yours was dead and has come to life; he was lost and has been found." A criterion whose measure is not human, a criterion that breaks the habitual boundaries of our feelings and calculations, a dimension that is not ours, to which we are called to participate, because deep down it is the only one that truly fits us.

Even more concrete and unequivocal is the definition of this criterion in the third parable, about the workers at the eleventh hour. The evangelist Matthew relays it to us, and he is almost violent in showing us the existence of a criterion that differs from ours, as the prophet Isaiah had said: "My thoughts are not your thoughts, and your ways are not my ways." The parable is about a landowner who compensates with the same amount the groups of workers who have worked different schedules. Thus, those who worked more complain that they were paid the same as those who worked less. And the employer responds: "Friend, I am doing you no wrong; did you not agree with me for the usual daily wage? Take what belongs to you and go; I choose to give to this last the same as I give to you. Am I not allowed to do what I choose with what belongs to me? Or are you envious because I am generous?" "So the last will be first, and the first last." The conclusion of this parable signals a reversal of our criteria, a complete overturning.

And this breaking of the human framework about love, this enlarging of the horizons in order to comprehend everything, and in particular those who are far away, is required because Jesus has only one commandment: "so that you may be children of your Father in heaven; for he makes his sun rise on the evil and on the good, and sends rain on the righteous and on the unrighteous. For if you love those who love you, what reward do you have? Do not even the tax collectors do the same? And if you greet only your brothers and sisters, what more are you doing than others? Do not even the Gentiles do the same? Be perfect, therefore, as your heavenly Father is perfect" (Matthew 5:45-48).

Another passage, from the Gospel of Luke, expresses the same thing in other words:

> "But I say to you that listen, Love your enemies, do good to those who hate you, bless those who curse you, pray for those who abuse you. If anyone strikes you on the cheek, offer the other also; and from anyone who takes away your coat do not withhold even your shirt. Give to everyone who begs from you; and if anyone takes away your goods, do not ask for them again. Do to others as you would have them do to you.
>
> "If you love those who love you, what credit is that to you? For even sinners love those who love them. If you do good to those who do good to you, what credit is that to you? For even sinners do the same. If you lend to those from whom you hope to receive, what credit is that to you? Even sinners lend to sinners, to receive as much again. But love your enemies, do good, and lend, expecting nothing in return. Your reward will be great, and you will be children of the Most High; for he is kind to the ungrateful and the wicked. Be merciful, just as your Father is merciful" (Luke 6:27-36).

At the conclusion of these two analogous passages, the words perfection and mercy are shown to be equivalent and constitute what God wants us to imitate. In both passages, it is clear that this precept must become a new nature for us that changes us in every way.

The third characteristic to underline is that this love as a religious imperative ("I always do what I see the Father doing") is a love that contains all its human components: sympathy, tenderness, generosity, service, emotion, with that human vibration that brings Jesus close to everyone and conquers their hearts.

We would do well to pause, reverently, at the twenty-first chapter of St. John, verses 1-19, when the apostles, having returned to their jobs after the death of Jesus, are fishing during the night but fail to catch anything. As day is breaking and they have to return to the shore, a voice from the shore calls out, asking if they have caught anything. And they answer no. That voice says: "Cast the net on the right side of the boat." They looked at each other, tired and disillusioned. Anyway, almost mechanically, they throw the nets out again: they are filled. "It is the Lord!" says John. Peter jumps in the water and is the first to reach the shore; then the others arrive. But no one dared say: "Yes, it is the Lord," because it was evident that it was him. And he was cooking breakfast for them: there were fish roasting on the fire. This is "God with us," this is God for us, a companionship that we could not construct for each other.

Let us imagine that strip of beach, in the last shade that was becoming more and more clear, that little group of astonished men, in front of a man who had risen: such a life, such a man, so timely and present in their concrete reality.

And the Gospel stories show us that humanity as one capable of affection for everyone, but in no way loving generically, a love that expresses preference and manifests its depth. Many times the evangelists underline these preferences of Jesus, signs of a true humanity: from the rich young man about whom Mark notes: "Jesus, looking at him, loved him" (Mark 10:21) to Lazarus, whose sisters sent Jesus a message: "Lord, he whom you love is ill" (John 11:3). This was so true that when Jesus came to the tomb of Lazarus, he was so moved and troubled that the evangelist John tells us: "Jesus began to weep. So the Jews said, 'See how he loved him!'" (John 11:35-36). Toward the evangelist John himself, who "was reclining next to him" (John 13:23) during their last meal together before his death, Jesus would turn his gaze at the foot of the cross and entrust his mother to him: "When Jesus saw his mother and the disciple whom he loved standing beside her, he said to his mother, 'Woman, here is your son.' Then he said to the disciple, 'Here is your mother.' And from that hour the disciple took her into his own home" (John 19:26-27).

The Law of a New Humanity

From all this, we can discern the attitude of Jesus toward us: he loves us and calls us "friends."

"This is my commandment, that you love one another as I have loved you. No one has greater love than this, to lay down one's life for one's friends. You are my friends if you do what I command you. I do not call you servants any longer, because the servant does not know what the master is doing; but I have called you friends, because I have made known to you everything that I have heard from my Father. You did not choose me but I chose you. And I appointed you to go and bear fruit, fruit that will last, so that the Father will give you whatever you ask him in my name" (John 15:12-16).

Here then is the great consequence of this friendship that "God with us" wanted to establish: we must imitate him, that is, re-live his love toward others.

John reminds us of the words of Jesus: "I give you a new commandment, that you love one another. Just as I have loved you, you also should love one another. By this everyone will know that you are my disciples, if you have love for one another" (John 13:34-35).

Jesus came to testify to the love of God for humanity, and he called us to imitate this love: this is how we will be judged.

> When the Son of Man comes in his glory, and all the angels with him, then he will sit on the throne of his glory. All the nations will be gathered before him, and he will separate people one from another as a shepherd separates the sheep from the goats, and he will put the sheep at his right hand and the goats at the left. Then the king will say to those at his right hand, 'Come, you that are blessed by my Father, inherit the kingdom prepared for you from the foundation of the world; for I was hungry and you gave me food, I was thirsty and you gave me something to drink, I was a stranger and you welcomed me, I was naked and you gave me clothing, I was sick and you took care of me, I was in prison and you visited me.' Then the righteous will answer him, 'Lord, when was it that we saw you hungry and gave you food, or thirsty and gave you something to drink? And when was it that we saw you a stranger and welcomed you, or naked and gave you clothing? And when was it that we saw you sick or in prison and visited you?' And the king will answer them, 'Truly I tell you, just as you did it to one of the least of these who are members of my family, you did it to me' (Matthew 25:31-40).

And St. Paul can write to the Christians at Ephesus: "Therefore be imitators of God, as beloved children, and live in love, as Christ loved us and gave himself up for us, a fragrant offering and sacrifice to God" (Ephesians 5:1-2). It is an invitation to walk in this world, which Christ has loved, with charity, and with the same openness that Jesus had, to give ourselves, offering ourselves in sacrifice to God.

To the Christians at Philippi, the Apostle says: "Let the same mind be in you that was in Christ Jesus" (Philippians 2:5).

Again, St. Paul concludes his first letter to the Christian community in Corinth saying: "My love be with all of you in Christ Jesus."

This imitation of God, this identification with Christ and the mutual love that flows from it, does not consist in feelings that we cultivate in the depth of our hearts but in concrete actions.

"How does God's love abide in anyone who has the world's goods and sees a brother or sister in need and yet refuses help? Little children, let us love, not in word or speech, but in truth and action. And by this we will know that we are from the truth and will reassure our hearts before him whenever our hearts condemn us; for God is greater than our hearts, and he knows everything" (1 John 3:17-20).

A deep love for souls generates the sense of mutual forgiveness, a solicitude for the poor, a sincere charity for whatever need, knowing well that the poorest are those in whom this need is stable, but that needs emerge in many ways and at many times in every human life.

We can find the details of this love already outlined in the New Testament. When the Apostles find themselves alone and after Pentecost understand that they are called to spread what Jesus had transmitted to them, and they build the first Christian communities, they have to fight, in all the circumstances of their community life, so that the "new commandment" is not forgotten or obscured by what comes naturally or instinctively. St. Paul gives us a particularly acute testimony: he was the apostle who united himself to the others later, who did not know Jesus but who with an incredibly intense vigor and fury strove for union with him, for imitation of him, for a life totally identified with Jesus Christ.

"My friends, if anyone is detected in a transgression, you who have received the Spirit should restore such a one in a spirit of gentleness. Take care that you yourselves are not tempted. Bear one another's burdens, and in this way you will fulfill the law of Christ. For if those who are nothing think they are something, they deceive themselves. All must test their own work; then that work, rather than their neighbor's work, will become a cause for pride. For all must carry their own loads" (Galatians 6:1-5).

"Let no evil talk come out of your mouths, but only what is useful for building up, as there is need, so that your words may give grace to those who hear. And do not grieve the Holy Spirit of God, with which you were marked with a seal for the day of redemption. Put away from you all bitterness and wrath and anger and wrangling and slander, together with all malice, and be kind to one another, tenderhearted, forgiving one another, as God in Christ has forgiven you" (Ephesians 4:29-32).

"If then there is any encouragement in Christ, any consolation from love, any sharing in the Spirit, any compassion and sympathy, make my joy complete: be of the same mind, having the same love, being in full accord and of one mind. Do nothing from selfish ambition or conceit, but in humility regard others as better than yourselves. Let each of you look not to your own interests, but to the interests of others" (Philippians 2:1-4).

"Owe no one anything, except to love one another; for the one who loves another has fulfilled the law. The commandments, 'You shall not commit adultery; You shall not murder; You shall not steal; You shall not covet'; and any other commandment, are summed up in this word, 'Love your neighbor as yourself.' Love does no wrong to a neighbor; therefore, love is the fulfilling of the law" (Romans 13:8-10).

"Welcome those who are weak in faith, but not for the purpose of quarreling over opinions" (Romans 14:1).

And after mentioning Paul's development of a lived love, a love "in deeds and in truth," we remember that sublime hymn to charity, where the indisputable supremacy of the "new commandment" stands in all its force as a religious imperative, shows man's participation in a value that is more than human.

> If I speak in the tongues of mortals and of angels, but do not have love, I am a noisy gong or a clanging cymbal. And if I have prophetic powers, and understand all mysteries and all knowledge, and if I have all faith, so as to remove mountains, but do not have love, I am nothing. If I give away all my possessions, and if I hand over my body so that I may boast, but do not have love, I gain nothing.
>
> Love is patient; love is kind; love is not envious or boastful or arrogant or rude. It does not insist on its own way; it is not irritable or resentful; it does not rejoice in wrongdoing, but rejoices in the truth. It bears all things, believes all things, hopes all things, endures all things (1 Corinthians 13:1-7).

This bold description of charity outlines a bewildering portrait of humanity: if we follow it step by step, every human criterion of value, even the typically religious ones, are shattered by being re-incorporated into a hierarchy where everything is annulled if it does not respect the ultimate priority: what God has revealed of himself in Jesus Christ, love and mercy, is the perfect, only law, which completes and gives meaning to every other law.

Conclusion

A profound revolution comes about in the person of Christ: the new humanity, the different humanity, different because it is true. Jesus is the first man with a true and perfect consciousness that his whole content as a man is the presence of the Father. Meditating on a few of the first chapters of the Gospel of St. John (chapters 5-8), we find a dominant thought in the words of Christ: he does what the Father wants, he sees the Father, he doesn't do anything other than what he sees the Father doing. The content of his awareness as a man was that presence. In particular, I would like to cite a few verses from chapter 8 of St. John.

"You judge by human standards; I judge no one. Yet even if I do judge, my judgment is valid; for it is not I alone who judge, but I and the Father who sent me" (John 8:15-16). And, a little farther: "They said to him, 'Who are you?' Jesus said to them, 'Why do I speak to you at all? I have much to say about you and much to condemn; but the one who sent me is true, and I declare to the world what I have heard from him.' They did not understand that he was speaking to them about the Father. So Jesus said, 'When you have lifted up the Son of Man, then you will realize that I am he, and that I do nothing on my own, but I speak these things as the Father instructed me. And the one who sent me is with me; he has not left me alone, for I always do what is pleasing to him'" (John 8:25-29). Christ, as man, is the culmination of what Abraham and Moses saw. Another moving reference that I would like to recall among the words of Jesus happens close to his death and is addressed to those who have followed him: "you will leave me alone. Yet I am not alone because the Father is with me" (John 16:32).

This is how we were saved: God sent His Son to show us what a person is and so that, in this way, one could find salvation. Just as the Lord had done with Israel, he got involved with our life, and it is impossible to conceive of a greater involvement than this definitive covenant: he became food and drink. The new person is thus called to experience, in Christ, the awareness of the presence of God as his very life. St. Paul will say: "As many of you as were baptized into Christ have clothed yourselves with Christ" (Galatians 3:27). And again: "In him all things hold together" (Colossians 1:17). "Reality is Christ" (cf. Colossians 2:17).

Belonging: The Truth of the Self

A Psychological Vibration

ONE OF THE characteristics of this new subject we have been describing is a particular psychological vibration that I will call the feeling of belonging to Christ, a belonging that is played out in his historical presence, in his body which is the Church.

We find in the New Testament, above all in St. John and St. Paul, the clear expression of such a belonging, whether in the words of Jesus himself or in Paul's words devoted to the first Christian communities. "I am the good shepherd. I know my own and my own know me, just as the Father knows me and I know the Father. And I lay down my life for the sheep" (John 10:14-15).

"Having loved his own who were in the world, he loved them to the end" (John 13:1). "I have made your name known to those whom you gave me from the world. They were yours, and you gave them to me. . ." (John 17:6).

"I am asking on their behalf; I am not asking on behalf of the world, but on behalf of those whom you gave me, because they are yours. All mine are yours, and yours are mine. . ." (John 17:9-10).

"Father, I desire that those also, whom you have given me, may be with me where I am, to see my glory, which you have given me because you loved me before the foundation of the world" (John 17:24).

"I made your name known to them, and I will make it known, so that the love with which you have loved me may be in them, and I in them" (John 17:26).

"Anyone who does not have the Spirit of Christ does not belong to him" (Romans 8:9).

"So let no one boast about human leaders. For all things are yours, whether Paul or Apollos or Cephas or the world or life or death or the present or the future—all belong to you, and you belong to Christ, and Christ belongs to God" (1 Corinthians 3:21-23).

"Not that I have already obtained this or have already reached the goal; but I press on to make it my own, because Christ Jesus has made me his own" (Philippians 3:12).

Such a feeling, or psychological vibration, is the most immediate expression of the ontological truth of humanity: a humanity that is created, formed, and saved.

Awareness of Belonging

God, the creator, made himself visible in Christ, and made humanity visible to itself, penetrated its existence, and moved it toward destiny. And this is the difficulty: not so much to be perfect, to be coherent, but to be ourselves. Life and time are given to us to become always more true, always more ourselves. If the years pass in us and over us, making us vulnerable to the power of society and to the human reality that surrounds us, all that we live, instead of moving us toward our destiny, blocks us, makes us perish, little by little. The kingdom of heaven is the truth of everything, and without this kingdom, everything perishes.

All of us have certainly held a newborn baby in our arms. Let us imagine that this little creature is already aware, as she will surely be in a few years, and we ask her: "Who are you? What are you?" The little one would turn toward her mother or father and call out: "Mommy! Daddy!" and almost automatically make this response. In fact, the nature of that baby is to be "of" her father and "of" her mother, until something emerges that is not theirs, her soul.

And when the child grows, she does not become educated in her deepest structure simply by the fact of sitting down at table and learning the rules and what she should or should not do. The child is educated and grows as a well-formed personality by the pure fact of belonging to her father and her mother. Of course, belonging is full of teaching and rich in words, conversations, indications, norms. But the child is not formed just because words are said or norms are taught; these alone do not bear fruit.

It is instead a total event of the unity between man, woman, and child that produces fruit in the personal structure of the child. Then words, conversations, and norms will be able to function as explanations, expressions, and instruments to help.

In this example, the event of nature assures the development of the child; but even for us, something analogous happens. The truth of life and of our person happens in our belonging to another: it is made of another, it breathes and lives because of another; in this precise moment it comes from another and is directed by the hands of another.

To become more and more true means to change our false consciousness of being rulers over ourselves and to arrive at the awareness of belonging totally to another. Such a change is not, as it might appear to the modern mentality, mortifying of our humanity, because we are made for this in our very origin ("If I accept my dependence, it is because this constitutes for me a means to give a meaning to my question," says Roland Barthes in *A Lover's Discourse: Fragments*); and the direction of this change—conversion—is toward joy. Not the perishable joy of a house that becomes a prison, not the equivocal and false satisfaction of being like everybody else, of having what and more than what others have. In fact, "Images and sensations, if idolatrously mistaken for Joy itself, soon honestly confessed themselves inadequate. All said, in the last resort, 'It is not I. I am only a reminder. Look! Look! What do I remind you of?'" (C.S. Lewis). The memory of the origin always leaves its impression in us, the image which the creative power of God first breathed into our nature; but it is the imprint of the new creation, of the new, the true man that God has revealed to us by revealing his own and our own face: Jesus Christ, who must be, if the world is to be true, "everything in everyone," as the apostle Paul says.

The new person is calm, open to the good and the just, steadfast, patient, capable of suffering, joyful about everything that is worthy of joy, when one knows that one belongs. A person is strong, a personality is active, a group and a people are creative only if they know to whom they belong. If our lives as men and women, if the time of our days and our years, saw the feeling of belonging to God mature, a greater breath would be experienced and everything would change, even our evil and sin. Because even if we are poor, the moment we say, with an awareness of belonging to him: "Lord, have mercy," we become true, and sin is lived as pain—not discouragement and desperation—that pain that together with joy is the greatest sign of love.

Being Born Again

Those who begin to conceive of themselves as belonging to another are so *different* that Jesus said to Nicodemus:

> "Very truly, I tell you, no one can see the kingdom of God without being born from above." Nicodemus said to him, "How can anyone be born after having grown old? Can one enter a second time into the mother's womb and be born?" Jesus answered, "Very truly, I tell you, no one can enter the kingdom of God without being born of water and Spirit. What is born of the flesh is flesh, and what is born of the Spirit is spirit. Do not be astonished that I said to you, 'You must be born from above.' The wind blows where it chooses, and you hear the sound of it, but you do not know where it comes from or where it goes. So it is with everyone who is born of the Spirit." Nicodemus said to him, "How can these things be?" Jesus answered him, "Are you a teacher of Israel, and yet you do not understand these things?
>
> "Very truly, I tell you, we speak of what we know and testify to what we have seen; yet you do not receive our testimony. If I have told you about earthly things and you do not believe, how can you believe if I tell you about heavenly things? No one has ascended into heaven except the one who descended from heaven, the Son of Man. And just as Moses lifted up the serpent in the wilderness, so must the Son of Man be lifted up, that whoever believes in him may have eternal life.
>
> "For God so loved the world that he gave his only Son, so that everyone who believes in him may not perish but may have eternal life.
>
> "Indeed, God did not send the Son into the world to condemn the world, but in order that the world might be saved through him. Those who believe in him are not condemned; but those who do not believe are condemned already, because they have not believed in the name of the only Son of God. And this is the judgment, that the light has come into the world, and people loved darkness rather than light because their deeds were evil. For all who do evil hate the light and do not come to the light, so that their deeds may not be exposed. But those who do what is true come to the light, so that it may be clearly seen that their deeds have been done in God" (John 3:3-21).

Jesus here invokes a new fact, a new person. Let us remember another occasion when Jesus placed before us the provoking image of the new person. It is the celebrated passage when Christ blesses the children.

"Then little children were being brought to him in order that he might lay his hands on them and pray. The disciples spoke sternly to those who brought them; but Jesus said, 'Let the little children come to me, and do not stop them; for it is to such as these that the kingdom of heaven belongs.' And he laid his hands on them and went on his way" (Matthew 19:13-15).

Now, what is it that characterizes a child? We repeat: the awareness of belonging. The Lord focuses our attention on the child to help us understand the most radical category of consciousness, that for which things, people, and we ourselves begin to have consistence: knowing that we belong.

We find the insistence on this regeneration in the whole New Testament, in the word of those who were the first to follow and testify to Jesus: Peter, James, Paul, John.

"[T]his life was revealed, and we have seen it and testify to it, and declare to you the eternal life that was with the Father and was revealed to us" (1 John 1:2).

"So if anyone is in Christ, there is a new creation: everything old has passed away; see, everything has become new!" (2 Corinthians 5:17).

"For neither circumcision nor uncircumcision is anything; but a new creation is everything!" (Galatians 6:15).

"In fulfillment of his own purpose he gave us birth by the word of truth, so that we would become a kind of first fruits of his creatures" (James 1:18).

> You know that you were ransomed from the futile ways inherited from your ancestors, not with perishable things like silver or gold, but with the precious blood of Christ, like that of a lamb without defect or blemish. He was destined before the foundation of the world, but was revealed at the end of the ages for your sake. Through him you have come to trust in God, who raised him from the dead and gave him glory, so that your faith and hope are set on God.
>
> Now that you have purified your souls by your obedience to the truth so that you have genuine mutual love, love one another deeply from the heart. You have been born anew, not of perishable

but of imperishable seed, through the living and enduring word of God. For

"All flesh is like grass
and all its glory like the flower of grass.
The grass withers,
and the flower falls,
but the word of the Lord endures forever."

That word is the good news that was announced to you (1 Peter 1:18-25).

Christ fulfills the historical trajectory of revelation, and in asking us to "be born again," he asks us to let ourselves be recreated by the Father through him who is present to help us on this path of definitive change.

Thus, every new form of relationship and of life emerges for us by recognizing that all people belong to God. We all belong to our Lord. The relationships that thus establish themselves are deeper than those that are born from flesh, from pleasure, from common interest, from convenience. And we can establish the value of every action by testing if it is or is not in function of the historical design that Christ incarnates. The criterion for every relationship does not exist within the factors of the relationship itself, but is determined by the same factors as our own belonging: the design of God which is *for* us.

The merciful goodness of our God makes everyone's daily life true, and this truth is always new, living water that flows from the foundation of the world, a new exodus out of the pettiness of our limits, a way out of the anguish of errors toward the encounter with him to whom we belong. Our life is a journey towards the eternal and a continuous bringing to light of our own limits. There is a way of living our limits like a tomb, a prison, but there is a way that breaks through our limits, not in the impossible attempt to eliminate them, but in the relationship with the only one who can overcome them. And so, the most minute things in our daily life acquire dignity, have a vast horizon, are no longer a source of tedium and suffocation, and become above all a peaceful responsibility, an apparently fragile nexus, but one that is powerful within that design that restores the person in history. The banal is not what is small or habitual but that which denies the infinite, a forgetfulness of the God through whom we exist.

The Condition of Passage

There is, though, a psychological-existential condition for this passage, for this Passover that is the path of converting our own consciousness to its belonging to God. To pass from the I as possession of self—as a will and a lordship over ourselves—to the feeling of belonging is a sacrifice; it seems like we are losing ourselves. Let us remember the prophetic figure of Abraham: the proposal of God was that of leaving everything that he had until that point woven into his existence.

Or we can also recall the encounter of the risen Jesus with the Apostles along the shores of Lake Tiberias, when he foretold a radical change for Peter's life.

"Very truly, I tell you, when you were younger, you used to fasten your own belt and to go wherever you wished. But when you grow old, you will stretch out your hands, and someone else will fasten a belt around you and take you where you do not wish to go" (John 21:18).

And we remember another episode of the Gospel where it was shown us that, if our moral consciousness is not one of belonging, it becomes formal, pharisaical, and begins to darken.

> Then someone came to him and said, "Teacher, what good deed must I do to have eternal life?" And he said to him, "Why do you ask me about what is good? There is only one who is good. If you wish to enter into life, keep the commandments." He said to him, "Which ones?" And Jesus said, "You shall not murder; You shall not commit adultery; You shall not steal; You shall not bear false witness; Honor your father and mother; also, You shall love your neighbor as yourself." The young man said to him, "I have kept all these; what do I still lack?" Jesus said to him, "If you wish to be perfect, go, sell your possessions, and give the money to the poor, and you will have treasure in heaven; then come, follow me." When the young man heard this word, he went away grieving, for he had many possessions.
>
> Then Jesus said to his disciples, "Truly I tell you, it will be hard for a rich person to enter the kingdom of heaven. Again I tell you, it is easier for a camel to go through the eye of a needle than for someone who is rich to enter the kingdom of God." When the disciples heard this, they were greatly astounded and said, "Then who can be saved?" But Jesus looked at them and said, "For mortals it is impossible, but for God all things are possible" (Matthew 19:16-26).

See how the attitude of this rich young man contrasts with that of the child, because the rich man possesses himself. He does not so much possess his riches as himself. That this passage is not only about money is even intuited by the disciples who ask themselves who can be saved. Material riches are here a sign of the possession of ourselves, as people who do not want to be changed, because to belong to another is a radical overturning for those who consider themselves rulers of their lives.

But let us remember the response of Jesus: this is possible only by grace, by God, by Christ himself.

When the consistency of our life is recognized as belonging, it means that we must be ready to make a sacrifice. To recognize, for example, in a relationship, that we belong to Christ means to forfeit that which in this relationship is our own project, our own hope, our own claim, to abandon this belonging to ourselves for belonging to Christ.

The promise and the rule are that whoever does this will find one hundred times more than he left behind. This is our hope.

The Hope of a Possible Miracle

Christianity is the announcement of the presence of God which recreates man's nature; therefore, Christian life is a possible miracle within the horizon of every day, of every action. And if we open the door, this announcement penetrates, changes, and reveals the nature of the one who holds the presence of him of whom we are made. Therefore, whoever lives this presence has a second birth; our flesh is made by God, is made to see God.

In front of certain events, our soul reawakens, while in everyday life it often returns to being flat, gray. We never put these two moments together, except moralistically: do this, don't do that, etc. This is not a new nature. Instead: either God is life, or he is left out on our doorstep.

The objection of our fleshly life, the unbearable weight of everyday things, has to be continually transformed and pierced, challenged by Christian hope.

The first step is precisely the hope of the connection between the awareness of belonging to Christ and the events of every day, because such a hope coincides with the possibility of becoming truly human.

Christ, to whom we belong, our salvation, lives within the limits of everyday life. We love Christ in the limit, and the limit *par excellence* is the person next to us, whoever he or she may be. This is how a new world comes into being. It has to do with a wife, a husband, a child, a colleague, or a stranger, the tenderness with which we approach the person who is next to us, whom the mystery of Christ causes to pass right next to us even for a moment. And this exalts the limit, making us live it as the presence of Christ.

"Tenderness is the art of seeing the whole man. All of his soul, all the movements of his feelings. Thinking always of his true good" (Wojtyla). Here is the Catholic genius: the Lord to whom we belong reveals his presence within the sign of each thing. Everything can remain wretched and laughable, but the revelatory and pedagogical value of reality is greater than the fleeting image to which the gaze of a person attached to himself would try to reduce everything.

Evaluate Everything: A New Judgment

The Cultural Dignity of Christ's Companionship

I WOULD LIKE now to draw our attention to something that comes up right away in the presence and companionship of Christ in our life and so adds a new aspect to the human physiognomy that we are discovering in God's revelation.

In beautiful lines from the Gospel of Luke, we read that Christ goes to the synagogue in Nazareth and reads a passage from the prophet Isaiah.

> Then Jesus, filled with the power of the Spirit, returned to Galilee, and a report about him spread through all the surrounding country. He began to teach in their synagogues and was praised by everyone.
>
> When he came to Nazareth, where he had been brought up, he went to the synagogue on the sabbath day, as was his custom. He stood up to read, and the scroll of the prophet Isaiah was given to him. He unrolled the scroll and found the place where it was written:
>
> "The Spirit of the Lord is upon me,
> because he has anointed me
> to bring good news to the poor.
> He has sent me to proclaim release to the captives
> and recovery of sight to the blind,
> to let the oppressed go free,
> to proclaim the year of the Lord's favor."
>
> And he rolled up the scroll, gave it back to the attendant, and sat down. The eyes of all in the synagogue were fixed on him. Then

> he began to say to them, "Today this scripture has been fulfilled in your hearing" (Luke 4:14-21).

Let us imagine what was revealed in the interpretation of this passage, what a disruption Jesus caused for the dominant conception, for the common mentality. He applied to himself what was pronounced in the history of his people, what Israel waited for from the Messiah.

The fact that Christ recapitulates in his person every meaning of every story is the center of Christ's companionship in our life, therefore giving the unique cultural dignity of his presence in every life. Other passages from the Gospel repeat this same situation. It is as if Christ were saying: "Everything that happened is for me; history is for me. I am the meaning of history." His companionship and his presence determine the perception that one has of oneself and of reality.

Finding the Reason for Everything in the Particular

We are amazed in front of the cultural dignity of Christ's companionship.

I would like to quote one of the most beautiful sentences from *The Imitation of Christ*: "*Ex uno Verbo omnia, et unum locuuntur omnia et hoc est principium quod et loquitur in nobis.*" "From one Word everything comes, and everything cries out only one Word. And this Word is the origin that speaks within us."

Christ is the light that enlightens everyone who comes into this world.

It would suffice for all of us to spend some time with this phrase from *The Imitation of Christ* every day, to deepen more and more our awareness of what we have called the cultural value of the presence of Christ with us. Because nothing can escape from the sphere of this relationship and of this companionship, nothing can be outside, nothing is profane in respect to this, nothing is impermeable to this. This companionship tends to illuminate and determine everything, because culture is a systematic and critical consciousness of reality, because reality can be manipulated and thus used in a way that is more perfect, more intense, more adequate to our humanity.

The sentence from *The Imitation of Christ* echoes the voice of another author, who was contemporary with the author of the *Imitation*, who in more lyrical terms says the same thing. It is the voice of Jacopone da Todi, with his cry: "*Amore, amore, omne cosa conclama*" ("Love, love, shouts all of creation"), where the word love is meant in its total sense: it is therefore synonymous with Christ, with the God who has come down to us and embraced us. The rest of the beautiful verse is similar to the phrase from *The Imitation of Christ*: "*Unum locuuntur omnia*" and "*omne cosa conclama.*" Everything together shouts the truth of Christ.

St. Paul says that he does not know anything but Christ, this Christ, crucified, flesh and bone, Christ the event in history, a fact. And this "knowing nothing" is not because Paul fails to care about the world, but precisely because through Christ he can know and possess the world in its truth. "According to the Spirit of God," as he will say at the beginning of his letter to the Corinthians, because only the Spirit of God knows the "depths of God," that is, the ultimate truth of all things.

And those who conceive of themselves with cultural dignity must search for the deepest truth of all things. What a fearful distance, and thus what an arid solitude, we experience when we compare certain great souls with the mentality that surrounds us, the mentality even of those who influenced the Christian education we have received. So our faith is fragile and at its root has a skepticism that can never foresee anything good, nothing in the name of which it can build.

Instead: from one word everything comes, and one word says everything, and this word is the origin that speaks within you!

This vision of our cultural dignity begins to appear natural within the context of the first chapter of St. John's Gospel. There is no other reasonable or practical way to think about our humanity, to conceive of our humanity, than this. In order to divide, to separate, to limit, to reduce—as Christians of our age have often learned to do—we would have to make an effort to be always distracted!

> In the beginning was the Word,
> and the Word was with God, and the Word was God.
> He was in the beginning with God.
> All things came into being through him,
> and without him not one thing came into being.
> What has come into being in him was life,
> and the life was the light of all people.
> The light shines in the darkness,
> and the darkness did not overcome it (John 1:1-5).

If this presence is the light that illuminates everyone who comes into this world, if the Word is made flesh, this presence must determine the perception I have of myself and of all reality.

So faith, the recognition of the presence of Christ and its continual renewal as the content of my sense of self, is to find the reason for "everything" within every human experience.

Thus everything is for everyone. The Gospel tells us in fact that "the Gospel is preached to the poor."

"For I decided to know nothing among you except Jesus Christ, and him crucified" (1 Corinthians 2:2).

"I regard everything as loss because of the surpassing value of knowing Christ Jesus my Lord" (Philippians 3:8).

These verses must not become simple recollections of phrases from the Bible but the very heart with which we wake up in the morning. We cannot conceive of a Christian without this heart, without this gaze on things. The Christian message is not based on persuasive discourses of human wisdom but on the manifestation of the Spirit and of his power—that is, on the event of Christ that remains in history. And the Gospel message tells us: the meaning of life and of history has been communicated to us through an event. So it is legitimate to say with Paul: I do not know anything except this event.

Christ did not come to teach us new rites, to start a new religion, to satisfy the human thirst for religiosity with different gestures, but to preach the Gospel, to announce an event. Therefore, we carry within ourselves and among us his presence, the presence of something that happened.

> But we speak God's wisdom, secret and hidden, which God decreed before the ages for our glory. None of the rulers of this age understood this . . . these things God has revealed to us through the Spirit; for the Spirit searches everything, even the depths of God. For what human being knows what is truly human except the human spirit that is within? So also no one comprehends what is truly God's except the Spirit of God. Now we have received not the spirit of the world, but the Spirit that is from God, so that we may understand the gifts bestowed on us by God. And we speak of these things in words not taught by human wisdom but taught by the Spirit, interpreting spiritual things to those who are spiritual.
>
> Those who are unspiritual do not receive the gifts of God's Spirit, for they are foolishness to them, and they are unable to understand them because they are spiritually discerned. Those who are spiritual discern all things, and they are themselves subject to no one else's scrutiny.
>
> "For who has known the mind of the Lord

so as to instruct him?"
But we have the mind of Christ"
(1 Corinthians 2:7-8,10-16).

Culture: An Introduction to the Whole of Reality

Just as Christ was in the presence of the Father and brought the Father wherever he went, so we "who have the mind of Christ" walk in his company. "The spiritual man" is precisely that one who is in the company of Christ and can judge everything because he participates in the energy of the Spirit.

This is culture: the introduction of the person into the whole of reality as an awareness in which every particular acquires its value. Such an introduction to the whole of reality happens continually through a judgment, which affection makes operative: because affection makes us adhere to things, and these come to be seen in the light of a total meaning. Culture is thus an introduction to the whole of reality.

We find ourselves here in front of a new definition of education.

The phenomenon and the value of culture are nothing other than the phenomenon of the human seed that is educated, unfolded in all its capacity and power. In this sense, culture and education are the same thing.

We are called to look at everything with his presence inside our gaze. Having this presence in our eyes does not reduce my field of vision that has the other as its subject but is rather a different and exhaustive way of seeing *everything*.

This is what St. Paul understood in his letter to the Romans: "Do not be conformed to this world, but be transformed by the renewing of your minds, so that you may discern what is the will of God—what is good and acceptable and perfect" (Romans 12:2).

This invites us to undergo a profound and radical conversion towards a new way of perceiving. Even we must ask, like Nicodemus did: "How can this happen?" And we have already heard Jesus's response: "We speak about what we know and testify to what we have seen."

As we continue to live the companionship of Christ, we participate in what he knows, in the things that pertain to "the Spirit of God." And we should remember that the things that are of the Spirit are the truth of this world: the mystery of God is the ultimate and truly adequate sense of reality.

But we, as St. Paul tells us, do not tend to comprehend the things of the Spirit—that is, how the Spirit of God hears and sees—and we try to manipulate the Spirit according to our measure. The things of the Spirit are absurd for us, madness, because they can be judged only by means of the Spirit. This perception of madness and absurdity reminds us of the shock that the apostles felt many times in their life with Jesus. On the lake during a storm, they see Jesus and think: it is a ghost. They meet him on the shore of the lake and are afraid. Neutralizing the presence of God is a perennial temptation for us. And right there, if we would adhere, we would discover that we are saved. But the shock and the fear come from the intuition of a call to be transformed by a measure that is not ours.

Salvation means that we are loved to the point that even our greatest misery is useful for ourselves and for the world. But it is possible that salvation may seem like a ghost and the consequences of salvation for my life like madness.

The Discipline of a Cultural Event

This introduction of a person to the whole of reality as its exhaustive significance—this introduction to reality that we have called a cultural event—happens through discipline. Discipline makes it possible for the cultural event to journey to its fulfillment. And the completion of the journey is a totality: "Everything is yours."

In what does this discipline consist?

Discipline is the only way to affirm life, to proceed toward this fullness, toward this new embrace, this new use of reality, this knowledge. To adhere to the presence of Christ in history without excluding anything from this adherence: here is the profound work of "culture."

This effort means facing *all* things as a subject who adheres to Christ, Christ who is a presence in one's gaze and heart. Facing all things—because nothing should be excluded, nothing forgotten, nothing censured. It would not be true "belonging" if it did not follow the orientation to understand the other from whom we belong. One does not belong to that presence except by following the impetus, the indication, that comes from that presence. This is what happens for a baby in looking at what her father does, in facing what she sees reverberating in the eyes and in the words of her father. It is because she feels that she belongs to her father that the baby follows the father, engages with him in docility, and learns from him.

Thus, immersing our face, our heart, our head, our freedom, within the reality of the presence of God, we open up and develop the cultural dignity that gives fulfillment to our faith.

One simple, yet deep, discipline precedes every growth, every spiritual and intellectual acquisition: *to follow*. This is why we have taken up again the comparison of the relationship between the baby, the mother, the father. . . . It is the supreme comparison with which we can understand the relationship between the person and the Lord. There is no situation, however complex, in us as adults, that cannot be illuminated by recovering an authentic image of that first, elementary relationship.

And "to follow," in its most powerful sense, in its application to the mature person, is to remind ourselves continually of the meaning of life, to remember a presence that invests every relationship with its true form of expression, of thought, and of affection.

The more one lives this discipline, the more one finds oneself caught up in a new mentality, a mentality capable of entering into any moment, following the various connotations of time, space, and conditions.

"Finally, beloved, whatever is true, whatever is honorable, whatever is just, whatever is pure, whatever is pleasing, whatever is commendable, if there is any excellence and if there is anything worthy of praise, think about these things" (Philippians 4:8).

This "whatever" is the most immediate and fascinating symptom of a mind and heart that live the relationship with Christ as a presence.

And again St. Paul tells us: "test everything; hold fast to what is good" (1 Thessalonians 5:21). Our truest value, our best judgment, can no longer be the enigmatic and confused depths of our elementary experience, an experience that can be messy and indecipherable from its needs, from its interests, and from its original demands. Because this experience is enigmatic, it always makes one uneasy. Instead, what makes it possible to judge, what gives life, is the gaze of Christ, a definitive word from God that has been spoken over our humanity.

Our position in front of the world, in all its expressions, all its striving toward totality, walking step by step through concrete situations, through the particulars where existence takes place, is this: to value everything in the light of Christ's presence.

The Place of the Cultural Event

It is of the greatest importance that the event that gives a certain intelligence of the particular be stable in us, in so far as it determines the meaning of our whole life. Let us ask ourselves about the method the man Jesus Christ used to attain this stable certainty. When he saw the sparrow fall, when he observed the lilies of the field, the hairs of a man's head, what gave him the certainty to use everything as a point to reach the meaning of the world? What made this certainty flourish in him was his relationship with the Father, his companionship with the Father.

Let us conclude by re-opening the problem of the relationship between the cultural fact and education. For us too, this certain intelligence is a relationship with Christ. But is the relationship with Christ at the mercy of our imagination? Of our interpretation? At the mercy of the state of our soul?

The answer is that the God of miracles, who imprinted his image on his creature from the beginning, whose revelation in Christ continuously reaches us and amazes us, reveals himself to us continually within a history that he made and is making for us, educating us always.

The genius of Catholicism is the God who becomes a person's companion in flesh and bone, within the contingencies of space and time. "Within" in the most powerful sense of the word—the most literal and metaphysical sense—which the expression of his presence in the world, the Church, teaches us. This is the genius of Catholicism, something opposed to much of Protestantism, which, while illuminated glancingly by the Christian event, represents an extreme level of human effort toward the divine through its own interpretation and its own strength of will, its own emotion. What scandalized the Pharisees scandalizes the intellectuals of every time: God incarnate, identified as a presence in space and time, and not as a metaphysical category. The Mystery of Christ, then, reaches us through a web of concrete facts with which he moves us, calls us, renews us, constructs us. Christ would be far away and therefore would be the victim of our interpretation if he did not live in the living Church; he would be totally subjective, in terms of content and of method, and thus would be unknowable for us, if he did not offer himself to us in the mystery of his body present in the Church.

Christ makes himself known, makes himself accessible, and gives us his Spirit in the Church through the sacred scriptures, the sacraments, apostolic succession, but above all his Spirit meets us and invades our lives through the entire life of the Church. The Church is the universe touched, enlivened, and possessed by Christ through his Spirit. That is, the Church is humanity made true, unified by the presence of Christ through the re-creative energy of the mysterious Spirit of Pentecost.

Thus, soon after the event of Pentecost, since the beginning of Christian history, the people who have truly desired to live the announcement that was made to them and which they encountered inevitably observed a very simple, mundane path. In order to realize their desire to face this fact, they gathered themselves *together*. In time, they formed not only the Church in her fundamental institutions—which permitted them to communicate the relationship of Christ to others—but they also recognized groups, movements, religious orders, and congregations. These forms of community constitute a factor of richness for which the Christian world should be thankful, not only because such realities have affirmed the freedom of the Spirit, but also because they are one of the fundamental expressions of human life in the Christian mystery. Associating with each other has always been the method by which Christians have sought to journey toward their destiny.

Within the Christian fact, it is through this unity among ourselves, in any way possible, but always with this tension toward destiny, that the whole mystery of Christ and of the Church touched and touches the eyes, the mouth, the hands, the body, and thus the heart, the soul, the intelligence, and the freedom of each person.

If therefore we have seen that Christ claims to be the exhaustive meaning of reality and of history, then recognizing our belonging to him pushes us toward a cultural work in which *everything* must be valued in the light of this presence that recapitulates *everything*: from the whole cosmos to every nuance of human life. But if we have also seen that there was a place even for Christ, in which every particular of his life and of his gaze as a man was determined by the total meaning, and this place was the relationship with the Father, then we know that even more so for us this cultural work, to which the consciousness of belonging calls us, cannot be lived without a *place*. And this place is the Church, born to secure our relationship with Christ, a Church which is alive because it reaches one in the cultural work implied by one's faith, in so far as it helps one to be certain of the link between the particular and the total meaning of life.

Faith as a cultural work needs a place where its judgment on reality is an attitude already in act and able to be transmitted. And the attitude behind every action is this: Christ is the criterion and Christ is here; he is our companion.

But our work does not consist only in grasping the initial shock of such an affirmation; our cultural work consists in assuming this affirmation as an orientation for the person, in looking around and seeing everything in the inescapable light of what has been transmitted to us. Investing our lives and the world with this renewed gaze does not mean holding back our gaze in any way: that would drown our work in a sea of aestheticism and intellectualism. The existence of this place develops the cultural work, leads it to take initiative in such a way that the truth of everything shines through our initiative and human creativity.

Ascesis: The Drama of Affection

Within the Horizon of God's Mercy

GOD, WHO REVEALED himself in history as mercy, wanted this mercy to become flesh in Christ and desired this flesh to spread throughout history in the mystical body of the Church. We have seen that the person has had the opportunity to discover their image in the progressive revelation of God, as a creature "belonging" in freedom, in the certainty of reaching fulfillment, the truth of oneself.

But we cannot help seeing the enormous distance between what is and the "image," a distance only spanned by the mercy of God, whom we recognize and accept as our teacher through the body where he is present. The mercy of God is thus the infinite horizon that gives form to the space of our life, a horizon in which the passionate work of judgment can work itself out, constantly poised to catch signs of God in the world and in our life through the companionship of Christ, the horizon of a great drama.

What gives shape to life, as we have seen, is the awareness that life belongs to something that is already there.

Let us go back to the comparison of the child: the child recognizes even in her physical features the signs of belonging to her parents. And we have said that culture, the judgment of faith, is the physiological expression, the reality of one who emerges more and more, who comes to light in a new birth. This something that is already there is the presence of Christ, re-creator of humanity, who remains in history, within the sign of his body, the Church, and the dramatic life that occurs in her. We are not called to live in this reality that is already there only with the power of our intelligence, but also with our affection. In order to become human, which is our destiny, we are asked to engage *totally.* Already in our description of the work of intelligence which judges everything in the light of Christ, it should have become clear that this is not just an intellectual game. We need to underline this, though, because we always want to simplify life and divide the mind and the heart, the judgment from the will. Therefore, we need to underline the fact that in order to find ourselves, we must remain in that place where the presence of Christ conceals and reveals itself to our intelligence and the whole of our affectivity. And here is the drama of our humanity that so clearly plays itself out in history.

What is affectivity? *Affici aliqua re*, that is, to be provoked to a state of soul by something or toward something. Affection is the human soul provoked to adhere to something. When we love a person, our very nature helps this process of adhesion through attraction, and then when attraction fades, we remember this as a happiness that we enjoyed. But it was not the attraction that made us happy; the attraction was the instrument of that comprehensive and expansive connection that is the special trait of the person who loves.

And how does this become dramatic, as we were saying? The drama is that we are called to adhere with all the intelligence and affection of which we are capable to the project of salvation which Christ works for the world; we are called to this in order to realize our humanity. But humanity tends to privilege its dreams, because a dream is every endeavor which we pursue outside of reality, even if Christ with his re-creative goodness can use the remnants of our dreams. Humanity cannot just undertake its own projects; it must become a part of Christ's project if it wants to maintain and rediscover its character as human. When one is aware of this, the drama is full of twists and turns, because we know that it has to do with our very existence, involving all the particulars of existence in their relation to eternity. We know that it has to do with breathing, thinking, feeling, in relation to destiny, that destiny that has already become present in Christ. The drama bursts forth wherever we experience this unrelenting drive, this direction. Because we cannot go against this drive: although one tries to hold it back, to hit the brakes, to forget about it, it continues to push one, to wound. As an analogy, we can think about the unrelenting drive that comes to us from the instinct of self-preservation. Because it is unrelenting, it is highly dramatic. To be marked by this drive toward our destiny is the same kind of thing; only a tiny minority of people are aware of this drive; and even in these, if it is not continuously recalled and reawakened, it disappears.

If this unrelenting drive is missing in our life, the thirst for happiness, the restlessness toward ourselves and our fulfillment becomes arid, prey to delusions and skepticism, and this progressive desert of the soul no longer experiences any drama. The curtain falls, and I am left with voluntarism or calculation, with solitude: in fact, drama implies the presence of someone other than myself.

A Drama That Cannot Be Censured

It is a vital task for everyone to understand oneself in one's depths, but when we try to trace the lines of our life by entrusting ourselves exclusively to what our reason can construct, we do not truly want to understand ourselves, because deep down we are not really willing to use our reason. Humanity has a latent, deep lie within itself. We want to understand ourselves in depth, not only according to the immediate, partial criteria and measures of our own existence; we have to be disposed to face ourselves with all our apprehension, uncertainty, weakness, and anxiety. Instead, normally, we want to avoid the drama, want only to understand ourselves and attribute a fundamental motivation to our life that is dictated exclusively by our own analysis. This way, we tend to censure boredom, tiredness, weakness, and misery. We would like to be free of them; we think we can obtain this freedom by censuring them, not thinking about them anymore. But this censure will make the individual only more arid and threadbare. We are called to know and accept ourselves first of all, and we cannot do it if we do not begin with our whole self. Jesus Christ, as the fulfilled image of humanity, as salvation for humanity, is the only reality who promised us salvation by promising us that *everything* in our humanity would be involved in this project, even whatever wickedness and weakness, and that everything could be transformed in him. "The doctor," he said, "does not come for the healthy, but for the sick." We can come to Christ without leaving anything out. We only have to appropriate and assimilate the reality of the incarnation and redemption in order to rediscover ourselves. "Christ is the appropriate condition which we need in order to think about and know man" (John Paul II).

There is a passage from the Gospel of Luke that has to do with the betrayal of Peter that is a fundamental and wonderful starting point to reflect on this divine welcome of the whole person on Christ's part:

> Then they seized him and led him away, bringing him into the high priest's house. But Peter was following at a distance. When they had kindled a fire in the middle of the courtyard and sat down together, Peter sat among them. Then a servant-girl, seeing him in the firelight, stared at him and said, "This man also was with him." But he denied it, saying, "Woman, I do not know him." A little later someone else, on seeing him, said, "You also are one of them." But Peter said, "Man, I am not!" Then about an hour later still another kept insisting, "Surely this man also was with him; for he is a Galilean." But Peter said, "Man, I do not know what you are talking about!" At that moment, while he was still speaking, the cock crowed. The Lord turned and looked at Peter. Then Peter remembered the word of the Lord, how he had said to him, "Before the cock crows today, you will deny me three times." And he went out and wept bitterly (Luke 22:54-62).

Let's remember who Peter was for Jesus the man, the one to whom Jesus had entrusted the Church, the rock that would guarantee his presence in the world; and let us reflect on the fact that he accepts Peter just as he is. Jesus had accepted Peter before experiencing those painful moments. Knowing Peter beforehand, Jesus accepts him, regenerates him. "The Lord turned and looked at Peter." He looks at Peter and forces Peter to become aware of his presence. To remember him. "Then Peter remembered. . . ." Peter could have tried to forget that regrettable episode, suppressing his remorse in a vigorous activity. Peter surely would have known how to do this, but that is not what Jesus wanted. "And he went out and wept bitterly." The memory of Jesus's words, coming back to Peter when Jesus looks at him, stops him from forgetting and begins to change him—already changes him, already inserts him into the dynamism of his liberation. Because we are not freed from our miseries by censuring them. And Christianity, which does not shrink from a realistic appraisal of the human condition, requires us never to censure anything, and therefore frees humanity through forgiveness. This requires a sacrifice; yet the sacrifice is never a censorship. In the ancient sacrifices, they took a victim and offered it up, saying to the divinity: "I give it to you."

Offering: A Gesture of Human Liberation

If we accept the drama of our life, of the presence of that relentless drive toward destiny, which ends the sterile and lonely consumption of our energy, our liberation finds fulfillment in the gesture of an offering, which raises us up onto the plain of redemption. Offering a sacrifice is a simple and synthetic gesture that everyone can do in whatever condition, as long as there remains a spark of self-determination in him. It is a synthetic gesture of morality, of love, and of freedom.

St. Paul says it well in two perfect verses from the Letter to the Romans: "I appeal to you therefore, brothers and sisters, by the mercies of God, to present your bodies as a living sacrifice, holy and acceptable to God, which is your spiritual worship. Do not be conformed to this world, but be transformed by the renewing of your minds, so that you may discern what is the will of God—what is good and acceptable and perfect" (Romans 12:1-2). Offer yourselves, the apostle exhorts us, your concrete reality, according to the totality of all its factors; in the apparent banality and in the powerlessness of certain moments—we affirm the whole truth of our life in this reasonable offering. This is how the event of redemption, destined to restore us to our fullness, vibrates in the consciousness of the individual and becomes operative for each of us.

The Factors of an Offering

There are two factors that make the gesture of an offering significant.

The first is that "to offer" means to recognize that Christ is the *substantia* of our whole life. If when we are studying or working, we can say: "I offer you my studies or my work"; if in a difficult moment we say: "I offer you this worry or this uncertainty that I feel right now," this means first of all: "I recognize that the consistence and the substance, the fabric of the moment I am living, is you. I recognize that what gives truth to my study, my work, to the problem I am facing, is your presence." And this is the true recognition of Christ because it is not an abstract Christ but the Lord who is within time and never leaves it.

But there is another fundamental aspect of offering, which is the desire that he be made known. It is as if we say: "If you, O Christ, are the consistency of the moment I am living, of the page I am reading, of the work that I am dealing with, of the sadness or anger that have come over me, manifest yourself through all of this." As Moses said to God: "Show me your face."

And God answered him: "At the right time, not right now."

In fact, the desire that he be made known is a desire for the glory of God to be fully realized, which will happen at the end of the world.

But even now, before the end, this manifestation of glory is beginning. St. Paul says in Romans: "We know that the whole creation has been groaning in labor pains until now" (Romans 8:22). The woman in labor pains is not like the woman who suffers without bringing a child to birth. The child is not yet there, but not having the child present does not equal zero; her pain is concretely different. It is like the sun before the break of day: we do not see it yet, but its presence invades the darkness with light, and it is light even though it is still night.

Asking: A Decision in the Present

In consigning ourselves to the God who can only be merciful, who always accepts us as we are, the reality of our misery fills us with questions. Humanity, as we have seen, begins the path of its truth not by avoiding its own misery but by offering it to the regenerating gaze of Christ. And in this gesture, which already begins a change in us, we ask that this change may continue. If he is mercy, we are certain that our questions will be answered. Because Jesus said: "For everyone who asks receives, and everyone who searches finds, and for everyone who knocks, the door will be opened" (Luke 11:10). In the horizon of that mercy which we know is a constant factor in our life, to pray means to bear fruit in our human nature in a creative and responsible realism that puts itself in front of Christ's love that makes itself an experience in time, in the present, where God calls and guides his creature with thousands of surprising signs.

The English writer C.S. Lewis recounts in the story of his conversion: "What I like about experience is that it is such an honest thing. You may take any number of wrong turnings; but keep your eyes open and you will not be allowed to go very far before the warning signs appear. You may have deceived yourself, but experience is not trying to deceive you. The universe rings true wherever you fairly test it" (from *Surprised by Joy*).

A Result in Time

A real desire to change is at the heart of our offering and our prayer, a desire which is continually renewed in the pain that comes from our awareness of misery. It is the pain that Peter felt when Jesus looked at him, a pain that is linked to a new security that can even make us cry, like the dawn of joy. Here is the heart of the new moral personality that we could not imagine before Christ came, the heart of a true Christian *ascesis*. It is not the precarious ascesis stigmatized by St. Paul in the Letter to the Colossians, when he speaks about many prescriptions "in regard to eating, to drinking, to feast days, or new moons, or sabbaths." He is referring here to duties and obligations in the Jewish law, not simply to deny them, but to put them in the light of "the reality of Christ," which shows that "all these things were shadows of that future."

Nothing is imposed on the new person regenerated by Christ; but everything a Christian does, she does in order to adhere to the unique reality she has met in Christ. Ascesis comes from a true love that brings value even to all the practical variations of life. Christian ascesis is not living white-knuckled in front of prescriptions. It is not wishful thinking or nominalism but simply the dramatic expression of a real desire to change which is dominated by the certainty that change will happen, even that change is already happening in the offering of ourselves and in our prayer for mercy, within the humiliation of our own fragility and error.

The result of this dramatic affection is a real result in time, just as the plant is the fruit of a seed.

Little by little, as life goes on, we acquire a sensibility to and capacity for memory, which multiplies our passion for Christ. This passion ends by destroying the obstacle, by shattering the evil which assails us, and then we are even more capable of following Christ and his commandments. All of this happens along a progressive path, a path that we call patience. "By patience, you will possess life," Jesus says. And again: "The one who meditates on the law of God day and night will bear fruit in his time." "His" time is the time of God's design, and the law of the Lord on which humanity meditates is the memory of his presence. It is an event, because the law of the Lord is Christ: the design of the world.

St. Ambrose said: "The saint is not the one who never falls, but the one who always seeks not to fall." The one who is truly immoral is not the man who never fails but the one who does not have this memory and this passion for Christ and therefore does not reach out beyond himself. The one who is far from Christian ascesis is not the one who never sins but the one who forgets Christ. The root of immorality is when we do not walk toward something, staying stuck in ourselves, even if we might be the noblest creatures in the world.

One Who Walks

The attitude required of the Christian is the attitude of a person who walks, who moves toward something. Because life is dynamic, it is natural for us to move, and Christian ascesis, the center of the Christian moral personality, is movement in the direction of what is adequately human.

Peace is the state of soul for this person in motion. This is not the peace that happens when everything is in order: it is rather the peace that comes from recognizing with the apostle Paul that "He is our peace" (Ephesians 2:14).

Christ's peace is founded on what God has truly revealed to us about being, what shines on the face of Christ: mercy. The experience of mercy is a feeling of what we truly are—so often complicit in evil—as well as a feeling full of wonder at the difference of the justice that embraces us: Christ who walks with us.

The specific form of this peace is gratitude, without which not even peace can last. Gratitude says that the other is everything and gives everything for me; it is an expression of pain and of certainty, the unrelenting dynamism of *homo viator* (man on the journey).

This person who walks is capable of always beginning again, without ever theorizing away or justifying his evil, but without ceasing to get up again, no matter how disillusioned or tired one might be.

St. John says in that wonderful phrase that should be the axis of every moral effort: "And all who have this hope in him purify themselves, just as he is pure" (1 John 3:3).

Hope is a certainty in the future based on something present. Therefore, it is the presence of Christ, taken note of in memory, that makes us certain about the future. And then we can walk without stopping, stretching forward without limits, starting from the certainty that he possesses me and will manifest himself in me. This is the ascesis of the new person about whom the New Testament speaks.

The most beautiful formula of the moral miracle that has happened to us is in St. Paul, when he says: "Hoping against hope" (Romans 4:18).

Ascesis is this: that the prayer for the presence of Christ become familiar in us, despite everything, in every situation of life: to Christ, a presence who saves. We must walk like this, without ever ceasing to beg.

PART II

A Decision for Existence

Recognizing the Evidence of a Fact

The Foundation

OUR EXISTENCE is first of all a decision about what we recognize as fundamental; such a decision is an event that proposes itself again and again. We must find the *unum necessarium*, the one thing necessary, which means the thing that we recognize as our deepest meaning and therefore the foundation of everything we do.

There is a passage from the Gospel of Luke that demonstrates the primacy of this decision about our foundation, about what comes first in our life.

"Now as they went on their way, he entered a village; and a woman named Martha received him into her house. And she had a sister called Mary, who sat at the Lord's feet and listened to his teaching. But Martha was distracted with much serving; and she went to him and said, 'Lord, do you not care that my sister has left me to serve alone? Tell her then to help me.' But the Lord answered her, 'Martha, Martha, you are anxious and troubled about many things; one thing is needful'" (Luke 10:38-42).

It is not an image we have of life or our own attempts at action, nor another person to whom we are bound, that adequately shape the contours of this decision. When this happens, we inevitably blame the uneasiness on the lack of a solid root.

Our foundation is the one who, as the mother of the Maccabees said, "calls into existence the things that do not exist" (2 Maccabees 7:28). He is the object, even if only unconsciously sought, of the recognition by which we begin to exist, to find our consistency.

In the Old Testament, the dialogue between Job and the Lord brings to light how much humanity, if it knows how to observe the world around it and the nature of things, must bend itself to recognize a powerful hand that rules life, a rule that is not any person's possession.

> "Where were you when I laid the foundation of the earth?
> Tell me, if you have understanding.
> Who determined its measurements—surely you know!
> Or who stretched the line upon it?
> On what were its bases sunk,
> or who laid its cornerstone,
> when the morning stars sang together,
> and all the sons of God shouted for joy?
> "Or who shut in the sea with doors,
> when it burst forth from the womb;
> when I made clouds its garment,
> and thick darkness its swaddling band,
> and prescribed bounds for it,
> and set bars and doors,
> and said, 'Thus far shall you come, and no farther,
> and here shall your proud waves be stayed'?
> "Have you commanded the morning since your days began,
> and caused the dawn to know its place,
> that it might take hold of the skirts of the earth,
> and the wicked be shaken out of it?
> It is changed like clay under the seal,
> and it is dyed like a garment.
> From the wicked their light is withheld,
> and their uplifted arm is broken.
> "Have you entered into the springs of the sea,
> or walked in the recesses of the deep?
> Have the gates of death been revealed to you,
> or have you seen the gates of deep darkness?
> Have you comprehended the expanse of the earth?
> Declare, if you know all this.
> "Where is the way to the dwelling of light,
> and where is the place of darkness,
> that you may take it to its territory
> and that you may discern the paths to its home?
> You know, for you were born then,
> and the number of your days is great!
> "Have you entered the storehouses of the snow,
> or have you seen the storehouses of the hail,

which I have reserved for the time of trouble,
for the day of battle and war?
What is the way to the place where the light is distributed,
or where the east wind is scattered upon the earth?
"Who has cleft a channel for the torrents of rain,
and a way for the thunderbolt,
to bring rain on a land where no man is,
on the desert in which there is no man;
to satisfy the waste and desolate land,
and to make the ground put forth grass?
"Has the rain a father,
or who has begotten the drops of dew?
From whose womb did the ice come forth,
and who has given birth to the hoarfrost of heaven?
The waters become hard like stone,
and the face of the deep is frozen.
"Can you bind the chains of the Pleiades,
or loose the cords of Orion?
Can you lead forth the Mazzaroth in their season,
or can you guide the Bear with its children?
Do you know the ordinances of the heavens?
Can you establish their rule on the earth?
"Can you lift up your voice to the clouds,
that a flood of waters may cover you?" (Job 38:4-34).

The main problem in life is our relationship with God. But even saying this is not enough to explain how much this relationship is constitutive of the I, the person. The question of life is the God who made himself an historical fact, the God of history. Faith is manifested in this way: in the recognition of his presence within our history.

Adhering

The objectivity of God's history, which we recognize through faith inside our life, is fully proven by one thing: by our adhesion. All of life finds strength in an "adhering to," an adherence that is fleshed out in the embrace of an objective situation where our consistency is recognized, where the value of faith is announced in a persuasive way.

We then live the rest of life with a totally different openness, with a changed color, within the ultimate objectivity to which we have submitted ourselves.

Jesus in the Gospel says: "So everyone who acknowledges me before men, I also will acknowledge before my Father who is in heaven" (Matthew 10:32). And being acknowledged before the Father who is in heaven means building something stable that challenges the storms of time—the wind is quick to sweep away the events of life!—something that does not succumb to destruction.

Anyone, in whatever situation one finds oneself, cannot but desire this stable fulfillment, however one imagines it or whatever name one gives it.

Thus, the most important topic for the heart, which is the stability of its own fulfillment—the certainty of our own destiny, the possibility of our perfection—belongs undoubtedly to that decisive proposal to which we adhere.

In fact, the certainty of our own fulfillment results from the objectivity of the history with which God made himself a presence and belongs therefore to the definitive form with which that story has personally included and guided us. The simple gesture of adhering to this form, to this web of contingencies and situations—the gesture of obedience—testifies to the wisdom with which the creative force of God's power articulates itself, penetrates and impacts our freedom. The truest moment of our freedom happens within the contingency where we have found ourselves, even in that place where we find ourselves in spite of ourselves. Because here our most fundamental hope is unleashed, a hope which is not in us, in our *doing*, nor in a place that we reach by our own ideas and feelings, our own attempts at creativity. Instead, we adhere to something that is so tremendously present, that has challenged and continues to challenge everything that we can create or that others—whoever they may be—can assure for us. We adhere to God who calls into existence the things that did not exist: not the God approved by our thoughts or our feelings but the power who became a presence in history, in time, in space.

This presence is hidden within our personal history in the form of life in which we find ourselves: it is hidden in this fragility, so much so that in our pride or impatience we can live within it without being aware, or one little blow can be enough to destroy everything. Instead, our wealth is the mystery present in that fragility and results in the attitude of adhesion, as the dynamic of our heart. The foundation of our actions, the fruitful criterion of our soul, of our imaginations and our decisions, comes from adhering to that presence. And then we rejoice in the certainty of a support and an indestructible constructiveness, that are not *ours* but that act in *our* life, because as the Bible says: "The Lord remembers his covenant."

The Curse

We must at this point return to the authoritative word of the Gospel: "Therefore I tell you, every sin and blasphemy will be forgiven men, but the blasphemy against the Spirit will not be forgiven. And whoever says a word against the Son of Man will be forgiven; but whoever speaks against the Holy Spirit will not be forgiven, either in this age or in the age to come" (Matthew 12:31-32).

To speak against the Holy Spirit means that we do not recognize the evidence of what has happened: because this recognition is the foundation without which nothing can be saved, without which everything that we make, even if it is good in itself, is reduced to dust and scattered to the wind. If it is true that the building of the kingdom of God on the earth is realized through the power of the Spirit, then it is true that we can really become living stones in God's temple, with our original contribution; we can continue a new and indestructible event in history only if we place all our certainty, all the energy of our existence, in the recognition of what has happened. And thus, we can build only in the measure that we adhere to the evidence of the fact that constitutes us.

Instead, we are cursed when we place our certainty and our joy in all of those things that are cursed by the biblical prophets. We must always remember that all the sadness, anger, and distress that manage to overwhelm us during our day come from the fact that we suffer the curse of those who put their trust in something other than that presence hidden within our history.

Simplicity of Heart

Another passage from the Gospel can help us grasp the right attitude, an attitude that allows for true recognition and true adhesion.

> At that time Jesus declared, "I thank thee, Father, Lord of heaven and earth, that thou hast hidden these things from the wise and understanding and revealed them to babes; yea, Father, for such was thy gracious will. All things have been delivered to me by my Father; and no one knows the Son except the Father, and no one

> knows the Father except the Son and anyone to whom the Son chooses to reveal him. Come to me, all who labor and are heavy laden, and I will give you rest. Take my yoke upon you, and learn from me; for I am gentle and lowly in heart, and you will find rest for your souls. For my yoke is easy, and my burden is light" (Matthew 11:25-30).

The image suggested by the first part of this passage is the attitude of a child, or the word "simple" as opposed to the word "wise"; something that is a strength, an energy, a value that comes before our performance—the original value of our creatureliness.

Instead, we often place the value of ourselves and of things in *our* expressiveness, while true simplicity is totally amazed by *another*, that is, by the givenness of things; it is amazement at what God has done in our life.

The child is totally amazed by what she runs up against. In her very first contact with reality, the child acknowledges what is given. And this is above all what is missing in our life.

The second part of this passage from the Gospel, "no one knows the Son except the Father, and no one knows the Father except the Son and any one to whom the Son chooses to reveal him" (Matthew 11:27), accompanies the attitude of the child, which we also call simplicity or poverty of spirit, an attitude that has nothing to defend: it becomes clear when we enter into that attitude, our simplicity and poverty bear fruit in gratitude, and from that gratitude a subtle joy; because the history that has led to our life is a gift ("those to whom the Son chooses to reveal him").

And in the third part, the passage says: "Come to me, all who labor and are heavy laden, and I will give you rest" (Matthew 11:28). This "I" is the history of his presence within the circumstances of life. He says: your complete rest will come by adhering to this story, to this definitive form.

"Take my yoke upon you, and learn from me; for I am gentle and lowly in heart, and you will find rest for your souls. For my yoke is easy, and my burden is light." What is this yoke? The word "yoke" refers to the contingent conditions through which the concreteness of life has called us. The genius of Christianity, of the ecclesial tradition, is that God, the Word, became a presence, placing himself within an ordinary, contingent sign: a man, someone towards whom it was possible even to feel aversion.

This passage is a true summary, because it describes the reality of our subject, of our I, in the Christian story. This implies therefore a setting in which the presence of meaning is *through*, and therefore *within*, our everyday situations. When we do not understand this setting, the banalities that happen during our day are only a snare that traps us, that prevents us from seeing Christ, the meaning of what happens, and that tries to abolish the mystery of life. In the end, we lose the realistic vision of Christ's message to humanity: the fact that the truth of our humanity comes to the surface *in this world.*

Offering

If we perceive the total objectivity that characterizes the content of faith, sooner or later, timidly or boldly, according to temperament and age, an affection breaks out for what we find within the sign.

When we perceive that the whole identity of life is caught up in the story that has happened, that this story qualifies the way we think and feel, when we understand this, when we truly gain awareness of what the faith really is, that it is the history of another—then our attachment tends to pour itself out on this other: "You are me." And therefore an affection for the Son of Man begins to arise.

The gesture that expresses this affection, that expresses and educates it at the same time, just like when the affection between two people is expressed and formed by an embrace or a kiss—it is called *offering*. An offering is the expression of our affection for Christ. One of the prayers of the liturgy says this: "In the simplicity of my heart, I have joyfully offered everything to you." And another says, "He makes of us an eternal offering to You." Liturgically, the offering is a sign that carries something else within it.

Thus, little by little, our self-perception brings with it an experience of the evidence of another, of a presence that gives consistency to who we are, that makes us say "I" ever more fully. The feeling we have of ourselves starts to coincide with the feeling of the presence of another, the presence of the Son of Man, of the Word who becomes Son of Man in me. This affection for the author of the story that constitutes my human face, and that has its adequate expression in the gesture of an offering, becomes a true experience.

This experience begins inevitably in the things and the moments that we take most seriously.

A Presence to Follow

God's Method

IN SPEAKING ABOUT pain, which is the human experience in front of which it is most difficult to avoid the urgency of a seriousness, of a personal consistency, Claudel says: "To this terrible problem, the most ancient of humanity, to which Job gave its official and liturgical form, only God, directly requested and solicited, was able to answer. And the question was so enormous that only the Word could satisfy it, not giving an explanation, but a presence."

God the creator and redeemer, in the originality which is his nature and in the mystery of the new life brought by Christ, does not know any other method to make us grow except by proposing to us a *presence* to follow.

As the Gospel narrates: "As he walked by the Sea of Galilee, he saw two brothers, Simon who is called Peter and Andrew his brother, casting a net into the sea; for they were fishermen. And he said to them, 'Follow me, and I will make you fishers of men'" (Matthew 4:18-19). "Jesus turned, and saw them following, and said to them, 'What do you seek?' And they said to him, 'Rabbi' (which means Teacher), 'where are you staying?' He said to them, 'Come and see'" (John 1:38-39).

In order for us to become truly wise, to desire, to be free—in order for us to become a true personality, which is the reason God created us—we must follow another. There is no other way, no intellectual effort or human cunning, that has the value of this method.

Jesus says in the Gospel: "You search the scriptures, because you think that in them you have eternal life; and it is they that bear witness to me; yet you refuse to come to me that you may have life" (John 5:39-40).

Going to Christ to have life does not mean to construct lines of reasoning but to follow him through the way he calls us. Only by following can we verify the Christian call and realize that the end of everything is truly the kingdom of God. St. Paul says: "For since, in the wisdom of God, the world did not know God through wisdom, it pleased God through the folly of what we preach to save those who believe" (1 Corinthians 1:21). Trying to do this by ourselves, attempting to call up the proposals of God before the tribunal of our own criteria, would be the grossest vanity: it would be the sin of Lucifer, which claims to find our meaning by ourselves.

Besides, nature proposes following as its truest method: the mother teaches the child to grow by imitating her. It is not for nothing that the God of Abraham and of Christ is the same God who made the world.

Life is a path and we must follow another who guides us.

To speak of *following* in today's world can sound particularly irksome. And precisely in a time when people behave in ways that are ever more standardized and rendered anonymous in the mass of humanity, we sense, at least episodically and superficially, the need of a true personality, the need not to conform ourselves blindly.

To follow does not mean to copy in a mechanical way. Following is a human phenomenon, belonging to the person, that requires the commitment of the energies that most characterize our personality—that is, intelligence and will—and that without a deep and free engagement will not find their realization. So, to follow is not a passive attitude, acting in a state of suggestion without knowing what we are doing. It must be a heartfelt attempt at identification with the deepest motivations of what is proposed to us, an intelligent comprehension of the implicit values in the suggestions that are offered. And following with eyes wide open, with lively attention, we understand and learn, we grow in the spirit.

Following cannot be an automatic gesture, a surrendering once for all, in an irreversible way, to a current: it is rather a personal decision that becomes a continual gesture of freedom. For this reason, the Christian tradition counsels us to say Morning Prayer every day: to take up again the conscious decision to follow God. Therefore, the fabric that makes up the Church's prayer at different hours of the days is constituted by Psalm 119, which is a petition to follow God's *law*. "Happy are those who follow a blameless way and walk according to the law of the Lord."

"Blessed are those who in their life follow the way of the Lord." "You make me wiser than old men, because I meditate on your word."

To follow, then, is to love, because it is the affirmation of another as the consistency of ourselves. The one who truly follows will never just follow with a spirit of rebellion or angry submission but with an attitude of security and joy. In fact, the more we truly follow, the more we are conscious of everything, we feel ourselves open and connected to everyone, we are able to partake of everything with a critical and creative capacity.

The Revelation of the Method

The beginnings of the most significant contact that God made with men demonstrate the revelation and the evolution of the great law of human salvation: following.

We find a suggestion of this method first of all in the figure of Abraham, who represents the first moment in the Old Testament when God united himself to his chosen people through a promise. "Now the Lord said to Abram, 'Go from your country and your kindred and your father's house to the land that I will show you'" (Genesis 12:1).

And Abraham left without even knowing the goal of his journey.

"And he brought him outside and said, 'Look toward heaven, and number the stars, if you are able to number them.' Then he said to him, 'So shall your descendants be.' And he believed the Lord; and he reckoned it to him as righteousness" (Genesis 15:5-6). Abraham abandoned himself to the will of God and did what God commanded him, in view of his promise. He had an only son who was miraculously born in his old age: God told Abraham to sacrifice him. It was a commandment in appalling contrast with the promise of numerous descendants. But Abraham obeyed all the same—"he followed"—he left during the night with Isaac, without even knowing where God would order him to make the sacrifice and without knowing that God would not make him carry it all the way out. St. Paul will note in his letters how Abraham was the anticipation, the person closest to the ideal of Christ.

The Virgin Mary also incarnates this adherence to the will of God: "Behold the handmaid of the Lord; let it be done to me according to your word." The only logic in the life of the Virgin was the mystery, the obscure light of mystery that she chose to follow: she did not have any projects of her own; she would not have any projects for her child: "Let it be done to me according to your word." And the wisdom of this Word, to which Mary entrusted herself, guided her from the first moment that event happened: she would continually look for its verification; she would experience its whole truth as it was fulfilled in time.

Since the beginning of Old Testament prophecy, the fundamental attitude of Christ was revealed as the attitude of one who is always available to follow the will of another. The Psalms portray it as "the servant whose eyes are fixed on the hand of his lord." The Gospel of John underlines many times the obedience of Christ: "The Son cannot do anything by himself except what he sees the Father doing; and everything that the Father does, the Son also does." And again: "I always do what pleases him." And when at twelve years of age his mother asks him why he strayed from his parents and remained behind in the temple, while they were worried and looked for him, St. Luke reports in his Gospel that the child answered them: "Why were you looking for me? Did you not know that I must be about my Father's business?" But how can a twelve-year-old child say something like this? Even for Christ it is valid for us to say what is true for every child: children repeat what they have heard; they begin to follow what they have observed. This great rule never fails. And in Christ, his abandonment to the Father also finds its human roots in the wisdom of Mary's humanity, a humanity that grew and was formed in her entrustment to the mystery by which she conceived her child.

Since the coming of Christ this entrusting of ourselves to God is concretized in following the Christian community, the Church. The Church continues through time and space the presence of God incarnate on the earth. She is therefore the great presence we follow today. Let us remember the dramatic conversion of Paul narrated in the Acts of the Apostles: "And I fell to the ground and heard a voice saying to me, 'Saul, Saul, why do you persecute me?' And I answered, 'Who are you, Lord?' And he said to me, 'I am Jesus of Nazareth whom you are persecuting.' Now those who were with me saw the light but did not hear the voice of the one who was speaking to me.' And I said, 'What shall I do, Lord?' And the Lord said to me, 'Rise, and go into Damascus, and there you will be told all that is appointed for you to do'" (Acts 22:7-10). Thus God sends an authority from the Christian community in Damascus, Ananias, whose instruction Saul, who was the fiercest persecutor of Christians, will have to follow, even if Ananias did not have the same exceptional qualities that Saul had.

Applying the Method

Hereafter Paul, as the apostle who would announce Christ to everyone, and not only to the people of Israel, expresses the concept of following with the word *obedience.*

Obedience means to abandon ourselves to following another; therefore it is the only truly complete sacrifice. Sacrifice is not necessarily pain and renunciation but rather a law that makes us great and joyful and which makes us experience, as the Gospel says, "a hundredfold, in this life." Following means involving ourselves in a living experience, which passes—as the Latin word *tradit* indicates, from which we get "tradition"—its dynamism and its gusto for life to us: it is a heart that communicates itself, it is the heart of another that starts to move within our heart. And primitive Christianity did not set out to change a philosophy but to transmit a presence, to make present what had happened, to make Christ present by sharing in everything, including philosophy.

And thus, over the centuries, the Christian community went on to form, within her monasteries, her schools, her universities, a philosophy, a culture. Therefore the presence that we obey is full of expressiveness, penetrates and invades every situation, reveals itself as a new humanity, as friendship.

The most adequate choice of life for a Christian therefore is that of applying the method with which the decisive fact of our humanity made itself clear. This event is Christ, God made man, who can become a present encounter today, an existential encounter, in which we can verify a proposal that gives meaning to our lives—by following him.

The great law taught us by the event is that of obeying the encounter with our destiny: we are therefore called to be and to follow a presence, building our small piece of humanity along the path of life, right where we find ourselves.

A Proposal to Verify

Experience

WHAT WE LEARN by following is the word *presence.*

This is clear in another fundamental word: *within.* The Father has gathered us *within* an experience: if we do not pass through this filter, we lose an occasion for our maturity, for an incisive and creative faith within that place where God has called us, the role God has given us.

When I first started teaching religion in the high school, when I would affirm: "You have to become engaged in the verification of Christian tradition," they asked me, "Why?" I responded, "Because you were born here." The Christian tradition is the first working hypothesis that nature has put in our hands: if we push this aside in favor of something else, randomly or willingly, we will assume that our lives are fulfilled by the fundamental criteria of chance or caprice. Thus, we will live our life without reason and without morality, unless over the years some conversion corrects us.

Similarly, step by step, the presence that gives us meaning must be sought and found within the setting where God has placed us, not in the sense that we have to close ourselves in that setting, but in the sense that the condition in which we find ourselves should be a catalyst for the way we see and do everything.

But how does this presence invite us to follow, this presence that calls us within the environment or the condition where we belong? The presence invites us to have an *experience.*

What is Christianity if not that God has made himself an *experience* for man within a particular situation? It is the message of St. John: "That which was from the beginning, which we have heard, which we have seen with our eyes, which we have looked upon and touched with our hands, concerning the word of life [... we] proclaim to you" (1 John 1:1-2).

"If I had not done among them the works which no one else did, they would not have sin; but now they have seen and hated both me and my Father. It is to fulfil the word that is written in their law, 'They hated me without a cause'" (John 15:24-25).

The Gospel often says that when people saw Jesus perform miracles, "they believed" in him.

But if something happens to us that sparks a desire for prayer—something that we might never have imagined—that sparks a certain religious interest or a consistency in reading the word of God, is not all this perhaps a sign or miracle and thus an experience also possible for us?

Experience as a Verification

Experience makes the verification of a proposal possible, the verification of a call to which we respond. The call implies the proposal of a truth that is so existential, of something that pertains so much to our nature and life, that we feel moved to recognize it with all our reason. In this experience, we feel ourselves moved to adhere to it.

To verify an invitation means in the first place to follow it with all the awareness, consciousness, reason, all the critical faculties of which we are capable.

This is quite far from an obtuse "trying," and therefore, the first condition of verification is clarity, honesty, a taste for rationality. We must be attentive. The Gospel says the same thing: "Stay awake."

It means in the second place to follow the call with all the energy of our will, with all our capacity for engagement—that is, with all our freedom.

A verification is therefore an act that is intensely full of those two principal factors of our humanity: intelligence and freedom (that is, an engaged will). Verification is not just an attitude of curiosity, much less a spirit that is poised to accuse and judge the potential defects of the proposal. Neither is it a mere multiplication of our participation in something in a way that is only material, exterior, and passive.

If we truly want to verify, we must engage ourselves with a clear and open attention.

To have an experience, we do not have to throw ourselves into many initiatives: the problem is the attitude with which we participate, not the quantity of participation; this is the true attitude for verification.

This right attitude in front of things, a source of verification, is expressed by the word morality (from *mos*, that is, behavior) and coincides with a true availability to what it proposes to us, the real call of things.

This verification, as we saw in the gesture of our initial adhesion, needs to be authentic. This attitude has many names: purity of heart, simplicity, poverty of spirit: the poverty of one who has nothing to defend, except the authenticity of his original humanity.

The authentic attitude could be described as that ultimate orientation of consciousness by which one knows how to expect something from life. Only the one who is ready and attentive can recognize what is happening.

This attitude is normally very difficult to maintain. It comes naturally to very few, to those who have a certain temperament and are called to specific functions. But even for them, if their purity of heart is not educated, it can become corrupt over time.

The work of attaining and conserving this purity of heart happens through educating ourselves to love things *as they are, because they are*: as the Christian concept of love implies.

We could say, interpreting verses 1-3 of the thirteenth chapter of the First Letter to the Corinthians: "If I speak in the tongues of men and of angels, but have not love, I am a noisy gong or a clanging cymbal. And if I have prophetic powers, and understand all mysteries and all knowledge, and if I have all faith, so as to remove mountains, but have not love, I am nothing. If I give away all I have, and if I deliver my body to be burned, but have not love, I gain nothing."

We must adhere to things *because they are*, not because I am pursuing my concepts of justice or something else. We must throw ourselves into reality with energy and a spirit of sacrifice; we must share in things in order to judge them, to catch the signs of their value.

Thus the only adequate way to verify the proposal of the Christian call is to convert ourselves to it.

We are called to an experience that must be carried out with faithfulness, as long as the proposal is made to us. A following which did not start out with the purpose to persevere would not even be authentic in its beginnings. One can abandon the Christian proposal only if one forgets one's own original needs, if one betrays one's own conscience.

True verification of the Christian proposal, instead, is experienced along the path of that ultimate and unique answer of which human solidarity and love are a foreshadowing.

We are called, then, to follow all the way to the end, because the proposal is made to the end, to the last moment. "'Lord, how often shall my brother sin against me, and I forgive him? As many as seven times?' Jesus said to him, 'I do not say to you seven times, but seventy times seven'" (Matthew 18:21-22).

Even if we walk without seeing, following will save us, as if we had already seen and touched. Therefore, there is an unforeseen unity between the one who is truly searching and the one who has already found something.

The genuine attitude of the man who knows that he does not make himself is the attitude of searching for his own origins and his own destiny. Even when we have yet to discover these, we feel the usefulness and the need to continue verifying this proposal for our life. "If we walked away from you, where else would we go?" "It is useful for you": we could repeat with the Gospel.

Verification is the necessary condition for a reasonable adherence. A blind adherence would not be constructive; religious adherence cannot be based on irrationality. It was said to the first Christians: "Always be prepared to make a defense to anyone who calls you to account for the hope that is in you" (1 Peter 3:15), and St. Paul says to the Thessalonians: "test everything; hold fast what is good" (1 Thessalonians 5:21).

Verification and Faith

Verification always reflects on its own past: after following for some time, we notice a change in ourselves, that something more has been given to us. The miracle of this change in us, which corresponds to the phrase from the Gospel "you will be given the hundredfold in this life," is a judgment that looks at its own past experience and immediately re-proposes the choice for the future. And because God is more faithful than we are, he will certainly make us experience the hundredfold here below again and again.

The change that has occurred, which we observe in ourselves—if it becomes "reason" for our understanding and establishes a motive of credibility in the proposal—does not have the strength to sustain us existentially for facing what is in front of us: only a vision of faith can really sustain this perspective on our lives. The verification confirms the reasonableness of the faith in regard to the past and leaves us confident in facing the present and the future.

Faith will be an authentic support only if it is a clear awareness of the foundation of what we are aiming for. Faith affirms a presence that certainly does not satisfy everything—because the goal of our striving is the full satisfaction that is to come—but faith already shows us how much what will come as manifestation, as fulfillment, is already everything in our present life.

The confusion and solitude we experience are only at the level of appearance, not of recognition, of vision. Because the power that made today with its desire for satisfaction, with its aspirations, is the same power by which the fullness of tomorrow will reach us.

It is the power of God that assures the presence of that for which we are striving.

Because this level of dissatisfaction, on the one hand, and of the ontological presence of a power that satisfies on the other do not constitute a contradiction but contribute to the correct training of our spirit, we must engage our own freedom in order to recognize the connection between the Christian reality and our humanity. This connection is indicated by the word *sign*. This word shakes us, because, through the sign, the presence of the transcendent touches our flesh.

But we can also fail to perceive this sign, this miracle; we can miss out on it by going off on a tangent, and then the phenomenon loses its significance.

Man's freedom must let itself be shaken by the miracle, let itself understand this word with which God calls us back from our distraction.

The certainty of a sign that we can always experience sustains life with the stability of a future hope: the miracle of the living God in this world is always imminent.

The Christian life *is* the search for a miracle, a miracle that becomes history, an announcement of good for us and for those around us.

Verification as a Pledge

A New Humanity

THE VERIFICATION of the Christian proposal must carry within it, in faith, the pledge of that full satisfaction that is planted in the present as a seed.

If the verification does not bring an experience of this anticipated fulfillment, of this *already* of the future, it is not a true proof of the proposal we followed. The Christian liturgy speaks of the "pledge of immortality," of the possession of the "first-fruits of the Spirit," of an initial experience of everything in Christ, where this "in Christ" defines a new nature: *me in Christ.*

The power of the Spirit can cause our love for this God made flesh and bone to become a reality for us, an affection for others and for the world capable of being a true creativity, an authentic fruitfulness in our life.

The law of life is not to have this or that but to love; it is love that created the world, that gives meaning to history.

If affection for others, for our brothers and sisters, is already the fruitfulness by which the affection of Christ for us and of us for Christ gives power to our life, we can say that this generation is the generation of a new humanity, of a new people.

So, the affection for our brothers and sisters is not a love for a single abstract individual, that risks never having a real face, other than the provisional mask created by our imagination and for the use of our instinct, but it has as its object a new humanity, a new historical reality.

In Our Proximity

This fruit is totally concrete and made of all those things that make up a person; it would remain a dream or a moving target, ready to retract itself at our every attempt to hit it, if we did not hold fast to another law, the design of God in history: this new humanity, this new historical reality, begins in a definite space, in the closeness of our neighbor.

The desire for a new humanity and our struggle for it would end as something vague and up in the air, where the object of action and its efficacy would dissipate like smoke, if the newness and richness of our being did not know how to reproduce itself in this proximity of relationships.

Thus, God chose a people that among all peoples was his *neighbor*, with whom he made a covenant, by which he made himself a presence, with which he involved himself directly: and in the covenant with this people, a new *thing* begins to generate itself in the world, to reveal itself; God showed his desire to recreate the world by creating Jerusalem.

When that new creation appears in history, that seed capable of giving true meaning to life, when Christ appears, we will learn again the importance of our involvement with our neighbor. Jesus began with a small group of apostles, and then his presence would soon expand through the law of proximity in those first Christian communities. Because the Church would remain an abstraction in the world if it was not the Church through the community of Antioch, the community of Jerusalem, the community of Athens, the community of Thessalonica, the community of Corinth, the community of Ephesus.

At the same time, our sense of the meaning of life would be totally vain if it were not made at least somewhat capable of generating—as the pledge of immortal life—a piece of the new world in that proximity where God has called us. Any affirmation we might make, if it did not generate a new lived reality in the place where God gathered us, would immediately become an ideology from the theoretical and operative point of view and an illusion from the point of view of the heart.

Our true neighbor is not only the one who lives close but those who are called *with* us, where this *with* must be defined in the most concrete way possible. The new humanity that Christ came to initiate with his resurrection happens in our gathering together as brothers and sisters, as "neighbors," in this bond that he generates and which unites us more deeply than flesh and blood—"those who are born not from flesh and blood but from God."

Only the affection that springs from the awareness of this bond can generate a new human reality among us, a reality that is like a light set on the lampstand, like the salt of the earth.

A Mysterious Unity

The relationship of unity in Christ and with Christ, even if it is not always an explicit joy, is always experienced as peace. St. Paul confirms this when writing to the Corinthians: "And let the peace of Christ rule in your hearts, to which indeed you were called in the one body. And be thankful."

St. Paul identifies this peace, the peace of affection for Christ, with the call to unity among us: "God gathers those who are scattered"; "You who once were far off have been brought near in the blood of Christ."

But this "one body" that we are called to form would be a kind of ideological ethnicity if it did not become real in the concreteness of the call where God has touched our lives.

Let us notice how that passage from St. Paul ends with this little verse: "And be thankful." This beautiful exhortation can only find a response in the awareness of a unity that has been generated, of a new humanity: the sign that fully demonstrates the power of Christ, the presence of Christ, is our unity. God would not be God if he was not able to make us one; he would not be God if he was not capable of recreating a divided, exhausted humanity within a new unity. The Virgin Mary sang out her Magnificat when she saw Elizabeth in whom the same miracle had happened. The Magnificat came out of the awareness that they were called together in the same design.

Thus, the miracle of our unity is a tangible phenomenon that demonstrates the power of God.

Affection for Christ generates a companionship: we can truly live only when we live a companionship; companionship is the truest face of our humanity. In a companionship, we see the primacy of a relationship that fulfills, that fully realizes us.

But the criterion of this new human generation, of this unity, is not in evaluating how things "go our way." The people formed by the God of Jacob do not have a criterion about how things "fall into place," how things should appear clear to us, how they should correspond to our acuteness of vision, how they should satisfy our thirst for expression.

The wisdom of this new humanity is found in the obscure light of the mystery, in abandonment to the mystery.

What really negates the possibility of creativity in us is the presumption made of our instincts, which want to be satisfied, or the presumption of our intelligence, which tries to dictate the form of things. Instinct and intelligence bear true fruit when they are used as instruments of another kind of wisdom, of another criterion—the criterion of faith. It is no injustice when our instinct, our thirst for expression, is not satisfied, because our whole life must be in the service of a path that God designs and establishes.

True justice is faith—that is, the recognition of the path of God—while the presumption of our intelligence and the claims of our unsatisfied instincts destroy rather than build.

It goes against a true understanding of the Christian God to imagine a power that bowls us over automatically, without the initiative of our freedom; in fact, no gesture performed by someone else can take the place of our freedom. This is the opposition between Christ and the Pharisees. The scribes and Pharisees expected salvation as thunder and lightning that burst from the sky. Because of the incommensurability of the divine power with human power, they expected salvation as an irresistible phenomenon.

This same thing lives again today in the common mentality, because the world's culture, even at its most developed levels, is nothing other than the amplification and imposition of man's instincts and his partial vision.

We would like a gesture done on command, a gesture established by our measure, that satisfies all our desire. In short, we want a God who is really us. This is how they spoke to Christ at the foot of the cross: if you are God, come down, and we will believe in you. But if the miracle can be done on command, the next moment God would call us to make a free gesture, and we would be back at the beginning.

In each of our lives, there has been a history of wonders, of amazing events, of clarity—a history that foreshadows our fulfillment. But our whole life cannot be summed up by the glory of those exceptional moments in an automatic way. Still for everyone, there has been a sufficient story of such moments, so that it would no longer be reasonable if we did not search these moments for the meaning of our lives. "I did these works among them so that the Scripture might be fulfilled: they hated me without cause."

Our Struggle and the Glory of God

The image of struggle is fundamental to the whole of biblical history. Even Christ said: I did not come to bring peace but the sword. Our struggle is between the affirmation of self and the affirmation of God, between the mystery as the meaning of reality or our own ideas. The struggle is a struggle for a change in us, a conversion, which cannot but break and contradict, even if in some way it contains the measure with which we begin and which must be sustained by the word of God, by the life of the Church. This conversion is real work and by this work our peace is assured. As the Psalm says: "In his days may righteousness flourish, and peace abound"; "He has pity on the weak and the needy, and saves the lives of the needy" (Psalm 72:7, 13). And the word of God, which became life and not just some letters on a page, is the adequate instrument of our education, and therefore of our liberation.

The beginning of salvation, the hint of God's presence, the effect of the Spirit in us, is first of all a sense of our weakness and poverty. To be scandalized by our sins, our limits, our pain, is our greatest irrationality, because through these things we realize that we are nothing.

Sin and suffering are the normal path to reaching the truth. In theory, the path of our limitation presents itself as a "back up" plan, because the main road—the more direct path—ought to be the transparency with which our reason perceives the contingency of things: the simple fact that things are not made by themselves, that God is everything. There is no more perfect rational point of view than this, and the height of reason is the contemplation of these things.

Historically and existentially, this kind of vision is impossible and provisional. St. Thomas, at the beginning of his *Summa Contra Gentiles*, says that human reason is capable of perceiving God's existence, but only rarely, after much work, and not without the admixture of grave errors.

In fact, the Lord normally uses sin and suffering to help us understand our need of another: the fact that we are poor. The supreme expression of this is the fact of death. And God's use of this pedagogical instrument is a spectacular paradox.

It is therefore a sign of the small-mindedness in which we normally live that we are so scandalized by this instrument of the truth.

One form of this scandal is saying that sin is not sin. We do not want to give in. But precisely this is part of the "world" of which the Gospel speaks: on the one hand it throws out a scandal, makes us depressed and desperate once we have given in to evil; on the other hand, it pushes us to deny that there is such a thing as sin. Our epoch is full of theories and of ideologies that explain everything: there are no more mysteries, everything is fine, everything can be explained. But there remains, or there should remain, the perception of an insufficiency: "What I am is incommensurable with what I know," says the French philosopher Paul Ricoeur. "Nothing is more backwards than a humanism that claims to know everything about man," says Borne.

Our sense of insufficiency is set in motion by the phenomena of sin and suffering.

The Bible counsels us: "Put on the robe of righteousness from God." Righteousness is that true design that leads to fulfillment, that will bring to completion what it has begun.

And then: "put on your head the diadem of the glory of the eternal" because "God will show your splendor everywhere under heaven." In our existence as well as in the whole of historical existence, the resurrection of Christ will conquer; liberation will happen. There is only one way to block it, to impede its realization: it is the vile distraction in which we live—the great obliteration—or the evil rebellion that we permit ourselves.

The Bible addresses our human reality: "You will be called Jerusalem." And Jerusalem is that great human reality which lives by recognizing the risen Christ. It is the living Church, because our personal liberation happens within her unity. The prophet Baruch comes to mind: "For your name will forever be called by God, 'Peace of righteousness and glory of godliness'" (Baruch 5:4). Righteousness is the truth of God's design for things; peace comes in living this design. But because existence is in a story, peace means to move toward this design, to move toward this design even if sin and suffering are not eliminated yet. "And glory of godliness": the awareness of our dependence on the one who constitutes us, the consciousness of this being constituted by another (which is the essence of "godliness") who makes our life "glorious." In the language of the Bible, glory means fullness, the happiness which we already experience today—that is, the first fruits of the Spirit. The promise made by Christ who was dead and now is risen will happen, the true promise made to Abraham. Paradise is already beginning within us and among us. To live godliness, or piety, means that our humanity is transformed by the awareness of truth, by the recognition of what constitutes it, by a poverty, therefore, that would only be desperation if it did not already experience now what fills and enriches it.

The Affirmation of Values and Practice

A Question of Method

LIFE IS A task.

If in our existence we kept this affirmation in mind, an infinity of problems would be solved and simplified.

Our task consists ultimately in the fulfillment, the total realization, of the design that God has for us, whose echo in our life is happiness, perfection, satisfaction.

There is, however, a problem of method we cannot avoid. We are made for the truth, but to arrive there, the fundamental question is putting ourselves on the right path. Arriving there, then, is a question of time, and impatience is the greatest stupidity because it risks making us abandon the correct path for other alternatives. And these detours make us lose time.

In our effort to walk in the truth, and therefore to put ourselves in the correct position in front of life's task, the method is this: if we affirm the right principles in a serious way, a way that is existentially alive and participated in, our practical life will change. The temptation would be to say the inverse, because it seems like the affirmation of correct principles is somewhat abstract. In reality the correct principles, the basic values, are the path, and we cannot risk losing these in the name of something tangible. It is not possible to keep saying certain things, to affirm certain principles with our whole being, without life changing in some way. These principles are the perception and the recognition of the divine. And if this process continues, it will end up changing who we are, in spite of who we are. The problem is one of time. Scripture says: "By your perseverance you will gain your lives." It is thus a question of patience. Eventually, we are able to say that it is impossible not to change in some way if we continue to reaffirm seriously certain principles and values.

The attitude of the "world" instead tells a lie precisely on this point: that we must be able to measure the result of our ethical efforts. Life does not change by saying: "Now I'll change my life"; this would exhaust us and cause us to despair. Human well-being and happiness are not a fruit of some mechanism, a pre-determined outcome.

Instead, discerning the criteria of truth is the simplest thing in the world. It is like a mother recognizing her child. And unless we are totally and voluntarily taken in by a lie, there is nothing that can impede the consoling penetration of the truth into our existence, penetrating even through the darkness, if we are open to look for it.

Of course, the action of repeating these principles must be true. It must not become a lie, that is, something formalistic. Then we can be certain that time is on our side, because it is the instrument of God, because salvation is not our achievement but rather the objectivity of grace.

There is nothing more realistic than the affirmation of the right principle with tenacity and faithfulness. And time will produce a change. This change that happens will be all that is needed to testify to the miracle of God in us. And here again, success is not the affirmation of what we can measure, but the affirmation of life's true meaning.

Here is the drama and the pathos of human life.

The truth of our life is the measure of God; we must get rid of *our* measure. The change that happens in time, through a faithful affirmation of values—that is, in faithfulness to a "following"—does not conform to our measure; instead, that change confirms the miracle that is happening. Fulfillment is a grace that we discover every time "in the end." The lie can also dwell in the one who, thinking oneself changed, says: "Ah, finally. . . ."

This tenacity in repeating—we know if we have only tried to do it a little bit—is a mortification. But the paradox is that this constant recognition of truth, despite everything that happens, produces a unity in the I, in the person. The unity of the I comes through the recognition of a synthetic principle, a principle that, even if everything dissolves before our eyes, time will continue to reveal. We may not arrive at the totality, but the total meaning is already glimpsed even by an approximate dynamism. We can recognize this totality even if has not yet arrived perfectly.

The path the Lord uses is simple, like the path of John and Andrew, of Simon and Phillip, when they started following after Christ: they followed out of curiosity and desire. There is no other path, in the end, than this curiosity and desire arising from a premonition.

PART III

Morality: Memory and Desire

Essential Points for the Formation of a Christian Personality

Premise

GIVING WITNESS TO the faith is our life's task. The Christian has a specific task in life, which is not the exercise of a certain profession, but faith: to give witness to faith, to give witness to it within a particular state of life.

We have our families, we have our professions, but *the* task is to give witness to the faith. We have been chosen for this.

John the Baptist, in his work as a prophet, proclaimed that salvation was already present and pointed it out to everyone: we can compare the attitude that our Christian task requires from us with his.

In this way, we express our personality, not as priests, not as monks, not as workers, nor as professionals, nor as fathers and mothers of families, but as Christians, whatever may be the activity that occupies us: affirming that salvation is already present, pointing it out, giving witness to everyone.

So it seems to me that the essential points of the type of Christian experience that characterizes us would be the following:

1. Christ Is the Savior Present in History and in Our Existence

Faith without life becomes useless and lost. Just as life without faith is an arid life, without an ultimate goal or purpose. And faith is the recognition that Jesus Christ is salvation present in history and in our existence. He is present like a wife or a husband, like a mother or a father, like friends, co-workers, and the events about which the newspapers speak, even if no newspaper speaks about this presence.

Salvation does not merely concern the hereafter; it has to do with the whole person, the here and now as well as the hereafter—on earth and in heaven. It has to do with both because heaven means the truth of the earth made manifest. And the truth of the earth is Christ, as St. Paul says in his Letter to the Colossians: given that "in him all things hold together."

Christ is the exhaustive meaning, the meaning of the clear, breezy sky this evening, of my person, of our persons, of the whole world. To affirm that Christ is the savior means to point out the path on which everything can be realized and fulfilled.

Time was given to us to educate this faith, to educate this awareness, to educate the recognition of his presence.

Christ in history is like the sun at beginning of the day, like the dawn. A man who has never seen the sun, who has always lived at night, would be full of wonder when he saw the sunrise. He would see how things begin to take their form, although in a dim and still unclear way. And such a man, even if he cannot yet imagine the sun in its noonday splendor, would still intuit that something new is happening, that the sunrise is a beginning: the beginning of the day.

The earth, existence, history are like a beginning for the Christian, like the dawn of the full day to which God has destined us.

In the Christian experience, the night, in which we find ourselves submerged and know things only in a tentative way, gives way to something that starts to give meaning to everything. The clearest proof of this is that this dawning can happen for the most mundane things, for everyday things. Thus even our routine acquires a dimension of greatness and joy.

This sense of meaning is summarized by the Christian gesture that in the language of the Church is called *offering*. In the definitive nature of this gesture, there no longer exist small or great things; rather, everything begins to reach its greatness in relationship with Christ. To verify this as an experience of life, and not just a set of words, is the dawning comprehension of what the resurrection means, that new world that is already beginning.

This experience does not mean that weakness and sin disappear, but that desperation is eliminated—that we can walk through the reality of evil and continually overcome it.

When the disciples followed after Christ and said to him: "Are you the Messiah or should we wait for another?" he responded with the prophecy from Isaiah: "The blind see, the deaf hear." It was a message that could be understood by the humble of the heart; it was deliberately not made for the clever, the intelligent, even if it was open to everyone. The year of the Lord's grace had begun: his message was hope, the possibility of joy in the midst of our earthly life.

Thus, the first point that gives the characteristic tone to our Christian personality is this: the living awareness that salvation, liberation—words that mean the same thing—are found in a reality that is already present in our life: Christ.

The opposite of this first point is seeking salvation—that is, the meaning of our actions and those of others, the meaning of time and of the world—by establishing it as something made by our own hands. This happens in our personal lives, for example, when we cry over our dreams or when our expectations do not work out. We delude ourselves because we have placed all our hope in human strength. During Nazism, for example, many held on to Hitler like one would hold on to God, and we could say that they adored him. The same goes for people who have placed, or place, their hope for salvation in a Lenin or in some other leader. The leader, in fact, is the incarnation of an ideology, a proclamation of hope that rests on the work of the hands of a person.

This is the alternative to Christianity; it is the position of the "world." It is not the position of a Christian, because the Christian is, by nature, set against worldly hopes.

2. The Reality of Christ Is in the Church

This real presence of Christ is located—is "within"—the unity of believers, that is, the Church. In the Church as Christ founded her: with authority, with bishops, and with the mysterious gestures called sacraments, gestures which involve the whole of life, because the sacraments are formative for all of life.

So to put our hope for salvation in Christ implies a judgment that this hope is present in the Christian community: in that part of the Church that arises in the setting where we live, a community that may be small and wretched, small and full of defects, because it is made up of people like us, but—if it is faithful to the constituted authority—always exists in service to the whole Church as a sign of Christ's path.

Therefore, externally, the method of faith is to stir up and live in a community, a gathering of people who recognize Christ as the savior and thus are a part of the whole Church, guided by authority. Christ as savior: not of the soul, but of the present and future life, as a path and a goal—as destiny.

The opposite of this second essential point for the Christian personality would be to reduce the relationship with Christ to a relationship with an image we make of him—an individualistic relationship with an abstract image, whose concrete connection would only be the words of the Gospel according to each person's interpretation or according to an interpretation chosen from among various methods of exegesis.

The presence of Christ is manifested instead through the experience of the Church within the community where we belong, whose value consists in binding us together and opening us to the whole Church. It is an experience of the Church in the place where we are: home, parish, university, factory, neighborhood, office.

3. The Awareness of Faith as the Fruit of an Encounter

The existential awareness of what faith truly is and thus of what Christ truly is—the living discovery of the value of our unity, of our community, of what the Church truly is—these are not the fruit of a reasoning process nor of our study. They are instead the fruit of an *encounter*.

Encounter means the event of the relationship with a person and with a community whose richness is so authentic that we feel struck by a light and called to a life that is different and more true.

In this encounter, the value of faith and the value of the historical reality of the Church begin to appear in a concrete manner (not one that is abstract or theoretical)—in a real manner, to the point that it provokes us to make a total response. Because when the person is really provoked, he feels the totality of his life put in play.

If it is not like this, if it does not have to do with a totality, it is not yet the discovery of faith but simply the knowledge or practice of some religious form.

We can say, paradoxically, that Christianity is not a religion but a life.

The opposite of this factor—a factor that reveals to us the character of Christian formation—is to identify our relationship with Christ and with the Church in a few established gestures and not in the totality of our adhesion, as if Christ and the Church were outside of the demands and interests of our life. In reality, when my I is engaged in an encounter, I am influenced and determined in everything I do.

This encounter has to do with wholeness, with integrity, while the opposite is partial, a partiality lived as ritualism or as administrative bureaucracy.

In fact, Christ is the whole of my person; the experience of the Church is the experience of my entire subject. Christ and the Church are salvation for me, and I am always the same when I eat or drink, when I am awake or sleeping, if I live or die, as St. Paul says; I am the same person who studies, teaches, and does everything else.

Christ and the Church are the deep inspirations that even touch the structure of my actions, of everything I do. And so, the encounter is an *event* that stretches to influence all of my relationships: my relationships with things and with people and even the way I look at my sins.

4. Constructiveness as the Affirmation of an Other

This deep inspiration creates a group of new, different human relationships with every person but first of all with those who recognize this inspiration, with the people that form the Christian community.

The community, within the particular features that make up the environment where it is gathered, becomes the place of a different humanity, a more human place, whose fundamental rule is charity.

Charity means that we tend to affirm the other and not ourselves. To affirm the other is to grow. In practice, charity is developed as an attention to the person of the other, as an intention to adapt ourselves to his or her situation. We take the needs of the other on our own shoulders, together with the other.

This makes the emerging community a source of initiatives, of initiatives without limits. These initiatives of charity produce a portion of society that is humanly more desirable: in which, for example, the birth of a child is a cause of joy for everyone in the community, the marriage of two people in the community is equally a festivity for everyone else. Or again: where the sick are helped, or someone who is kicked out of his family can fall on the shoulders of the whole community, within the limits of what is possible and according to the freedom of each member. I am not only speaking about an ideal but of things that, in the Christian community, really happen.

The world and society change through human realities that have already been changed. But we must remember that a truly new change can only come from outside us, from an other, radically different than us. This is the grace of the presence of Christ recognized and loved in the mystery of his Church. This grace takes on the everyday form of the ecclesial community where we live.

The opposite of this fourth point is moralism.

Moralism is thinking that we can be just by applying laws of behavior, doing good according to our own instinct or our own conception, passing over those who are closest to us, our neighbors.

Our neighbor is, in the first place, the one whom Christ has put next to us. There is no greater neighbor than the one who like us recognizes Christ as savior: our brothers and sisters in the community.

Through these brothers and sisters, through the human experience of community, as it unfolds, we become capable of something more than human—more just, more able to take the initiative, even with those that are outside of the community, with the whole society, where the poor require our attention in a preferential way. It is like a rock that falls in a pond and produces concentric circles that go out, always widening and multiplying. But the point of departure must not be forgotten. The point of departure is found in those whom Christ puts at our side, puts close to us: our brothers and sisters in faith.

In the moralistic attitude, the starting point for us is the opinion or the project developed by our own consciousness.

5. The Community, a Place of Faith in the World

As I said earlier, the Christian community, which is the place of faith, lives within the body of society: it is in the world, it is a part of this society, of this world, and experiences the same problems as everyone else.

The community gets involved either by intervening directly in certain problems or by educating its members so that they can responsibly and personally intervene.

For that reason, the sign of a living Christian community is that in the awareness of its faith in Christ and in the awareness of its belonging to the Church, this community confronts all the problems of society, either directly or through the engagement of its individual members.

Two fundamental aspects mark this engagement.

The first is that the solution to a problem is false, is illusory, if it does not respect the values of the ecclesial community, the values by which the community lives: the conception of humanity that the Church has, the sense of history that the Church proposes.

The second is that the awareness of belonging to the community—the awareness of our unity, of our communion—is a determining factor of the same consciousness with which the Christian faces, even as an individual, the problems of society. The community is the ideal point of reference that illuminates the conscience of the individual Christian, with which he faces the problems that are presented to him, or with which he shares the intentions of other people of good will.

The opposite of this fifth point has two aspects.

On one hand, we can conceive of the Christian life as a closing in on itself, without an effect on social problems, without a reference to the context in which we live.

On the other hand, we can reduce the influence of faith and of the Church in its socio-political action to an extrinsic impulse, to a simple inspiration, as if the ecclesial experience urged everybody to become interested in social problems, inculcating an ethical impulse in them toward these problems, but without being able to influence their way of facing those same problems.

This is very important today. For example, it is said: "The Gospel moves me to be concerned about the poor." This is certainly true, but if one stops here, then the Gospel tends to be only an ethical impulse, something moralistic. Instead, the Gospel has something to say also about the way—about the structure of judgment and of behavior—with which one faces the problem of poverty.

In a certain city, there was a conference entitled: "The Christian and the Marxist." Who is the true Christian? One who does justice for the poor. Who is the Marxist? One who does justice for the poor. Therefore, today's Christian should be a Marxist. This was the idea put forward so often in those years by many people. An old woman attending the conference raised her hand and timidly asked: "So what is the difference?" The people at the conference, after remaining perplexed for a few moments, responded: "The Christian sees Christ in the poor person, and the Marxist doesn't." Another friend who was present raised his hand and said: "Then I would say that the Christian is a visionary."

We should reflect on this episode, because that man's answer is significant. If Christ does not change the way in which we confront human problems, Christ is just a fantasy. Dualism, which divides us into a religious or a Christian person on the one hand and a civil or a political person on the other, is one of the greatest errors of today, in my opinion. Many baptized people live this dualistic position, by which the Christian is "Christian" at determined moments, in determined activities, fundamentally religious activities, but whose faith remains, the rest of the time, in the best-case scenario, a vague ethical impulse. In every other activity, the Christian is "a person like any other."

Instead, the newness in the world that is faith, maintained within an authentic experience of community life, fills the whole of life, creates a different subject, a new "creature." And the totality of this person's activity, her judgment on things, her vision of humanity and of history, her relationships and her behavior, cannot cease to be determined and qualified by this faith.

Faith fills our entire life, and it is a proposal for our life every day.

Conclusion

I think that these five points, along with their opposites, can help us work to discover a Christian life that is alive and formative, capable of acknowledging our condition as sinful beings on the one hand and as children of our time on the other.

To live this new life, we need only grace and poverty of spirit; we need to recognize the presence that is in the world.

The saints, in fact, are those who recognize the plan of God, which is the presence of Christ, and, through following this presence, cooperate together for the good of humanity according to its deepest and most authentic destiny. While all ideologies build themselves on the ruins of scandal and violence, Christian newness is the peaceful miracle of a person who risks everything on a life in the Church.

A thousand years ago, a man traveled on the back of a mule and could be more human and happy than a man today who cuts across the sky on board a jet. "Progress" is desirable, but the human good is not necessarily identified with the development of technological civilization, which can even prove itself counterproductive to human civility. In fact, this civilization has built a great many ways to alienate our humanity.

The principal problem is our humanization, the truth of the person. The Christian community collaborates in this task by educating people in the faith. This is the best instrument for creating subjects who can employ technological civilization *for* the person. By saying "Your Kingdom come," we are praying for salvation in this world.

This is the ideal, and it is the opposite of any utopian dream, of any image created by human beings. The ideal ends up transforming, sooner or later, every step of the human journey. Therefore, the ideal is the most concrete thing that exists.

This ideal is a life of faith, a faith that touches our whole life.

Prayer

Prayer: Awareness of Our Dependence

1.

SAINT AUGUSTINE defined prayer as *Elevatio mentis in Deum.*

We could translate this as: "To become aware of God."

But what does it mean to become aware of God? In the deepest sense, becoming aware of God means to recognize our original dependence. Not simply a dependence in the past, in that act by which God created us—like when a son, born "by the will of the flesh," thinks of his father—but a total dependence, in every instant, continuously, in every gesture. In every instance, every gesture of our existence has its origin in the mystery of Being; there is our true Father, the Father of that continual generation which is our existence. *Tam Pater, nemo* ("No one is a Father like he is").

We are distinguished from other creatures inasmuch as we are aware of that by which we live; this consciousness is not complete if it does not touch the foundation from which it arises; the arc of reflection does not realize its fullest dimensions if it does not arrive at the point from which the I with all its gestures breaks forth. The ideal person—a person who is completely realized—should possess this uninterrupted awareness. Jesus said, "Pray always."

But this awareness, except for a very particular grace and therefore a very particular function, is impossible for us. The transparency of the presence of our own being is normally opaque. We find ourselves truly—that is, we see ourselves according to this dependence on God—only intermittently, more or less frequently. The ideal which Jesus dreamed of can be translated existentially like this: "pray more than you can." It is the formula of a conscience in front of the ideal; it is the formula of freedom for one who is on a journey. It is a formula that comprises our entire existence, with all its various limitations and the mutability of its conditions, and at the same time is a formula that inexorably affirms the incessant demand of a duty, whose call no limit or condition can silence.

2.

Consciousness of such dependence, in the measure in which it is known and participated in, does not remain a purely intellectual event. We have an irresistible vocation to live, to be: therefore the awareness that one's life is integrally dependent on God, like a stream on its source, becomes a question. So the definition of prayer given by St. Augustine coincides with that given by St. Thomas: *Petitio decentium a Deo*—asking God the appropriate things. But what are all of these "appropriate things" if not "being," the realization of self, the completion of that design for which we were made?

Asking for being, this is how prayer becomes an act of life: the demand for authentic "being," the actualization of the true I. "Your kingdom come, your will be done": his kingdom, his will is exactly, as regards me, the actualization of that idea with which he created me. Every prayer, if we want to use another word, is an asking for holiness: "Your kingdom come."

3.

Even when we ask for the most contingent and material things, prayer, in the ultimate analysis, asks for the kingdom—that first of all in me his kingdom will come to pass—that the I *be* what it should be, what he desires. It is as if one said: "Lord, I ask you for this, because it seems useful for my self-realization; but, clearly, I ask you for what is right and truly useful, not what seems such to me; because I ask for the kingdom, not things as they appear to me." This is the prayer of Jesus: "Father, if it is possible, let this cup pass from me; even so not my will, but your will be done."

A prayer that does not have this clause, implicitly or explicitly, would not be an asking but an attempt at imposition; it would not be an expression of an awareness of dependence but a rebellion. It would be an absurd pretense to constrict God to our measure; to make the eternal succumb to the ephemeral, infinite wisdom to childish caprice.

4.

Like every spiritual reality in this world, so also prayer happens in the humility of a few material, "technical," conditions. Let's list a few of them:

a. The first condition for accomplishing the duty of prayer is the same condition for every earthly expression of the person: *time*. We could even say that "giving a bit of time" to God is already in itself prayer. This piece of time set apart, "decided on" for him, symbolic of our dependence on him, can constitute in itself a form of prayer, especially when the soul is empty of its expressive capacity, because of ineptitude, dryness, tiredness.

b. The problem then arises of how to fill this bit of time. And it is filled with one of the forms of expression at man's disposal: *thought, word, gesture*.

Pure thought, done through a mental discourse, is a genuine prayer (*meditation*). In particular, the conscious gaze, fixed on the attractiveness of a truth about God, or on the very person of God, or on a symbol that reminds us of him, is the highest form of personal prayer (*contemplation*).

A word is the normal expressive instrument of the awareness of the I. This arises in an extremely personal way. Speaking with God is therefore part of the genius of the person: and it can give voice to whatever interest a person feels, because every interest is in the end part of the life story that God is guiding.

Gestures also accompany the awareness of an idea or a feeling: the person is a unity. Thus even in prayer the translation of interior awareness into activity and physical action can be a sign of fullness, not of childishness or primitivism.

After all, there are expressions of feeling that can become even more expressive through gestures than through words.

c. But we are weak, incoherent. While knowing our duty, we don't carry it out, because our will is lacking; or we are unable to carry it out, because we feel ourselves incapable.

It is possible, then, to understand the value of *formal* prayer *(fixed words)* or rites *(fixed gestures)*.

When we are dry or tired or incapable, using formulas or participating in rites puts us in communication with that original religious experience that is crystalized in a formula or a rite and a bit of that original warmth is communicated to us. Thus, each of us knows from experience the restorative value of an Our Father said slowly: the Our Father is the formula in which the religious experience of Jesus himself is fixed, and it is not possible to come in contact with it without feeling its warmth. If not even the ruins of ancient buildings can leave the one who sees them unmoved, how much more should these edifices of words and gestures not influence us for the better, discovered as they are by the creative spirit of a soul enamored with God.

Furthermore, there are formulas and rites that are so fitting as expressions of feeling that normally the spirit feels itself incapable of finding others. Even in civil life, formulas like "Good morning" or "Hello" or "Goodbye" are so clear in their synthesis that we feel them to be irreplaceable.

An awareness of dependence that refused to become asking—to incarnate itself in time and in action—would no longer be prayer, relationship with Being; it would be to give in to nothingness, an alibi for neglecting our commitment.

Prayer and the Communal Spirit

1.

ONE OF THE human conditions assumed by prayer is its communal expression.

It would seem that prayer, coming from the holiness of the most intimate conscience of the person, would be diminished in its personal originality—its purity, sincerity, and intensity—every time it was channeled into communal forms. This is the objection to which secularism has habituated us. But it is also a somewhat unconscious and confused conviction of many devoted souls, who see communal prayer almost exclusively as a limit, which must be adopted with the greatest good will possible, like a mortification of one's personality, an inevitable mortification for earthly existence, a holy mortification like so many others, but substantially a mortification.

This is profoundly wrong. Communal prayer is surely a mortification, like every other duty in this life, like every ideal expressed in time. But communal prayer is not only not a limit to personal experience—it realizes personal experience to its fullest extent.

2.

In order to understand this well, we need to experience the difference between collectivity and community.

a. Collectivity derives from a *situation* that a person undergoes. It is a group, a gathering of individuals, kept together by a criterion that does not coincide with their I, with their conscience, with their will—a criterion that is imposed on the I from outside, so to speak, which obliges a person, which binds him or her, as a condition. Interest, taste, convenience, not being able to do without, etc.: these are all criteria that can oblige the I to accept a life together with others, with their conditions, their norms, their laws. What determines and keeps the collective together is not so much the person—the I that participates—as something to which the I must adapt in order to live and to express itself at least a little bit; it is a *calculation*, whose social codification is *law*.

The collective is ruled by law, and its ideal is justice—that is, the measure, the calculation of equilibrium, that allows singular participants to live together with the least amount of limitation possible.

The inevitable condition of the collective is that the individual sooner or later feels limited, coerced. The condition of the collective is the anguish of the individual; sooner or later one feels oneself a prisoner, denied freedom, and begins to feel treated like an object, like a thing.

b. Community, in a way that is truly contrary, is born from the *action* of the I, from the expression of personal liberty.

Let's take the example of everyday human activity: physical presence creates physical relationships with those around us, and if this presence moves somewhere else, it creates other physical relationships: we call *place* the gathering of these corporeal, material relationships.

But even man's spiritual action, his personal action, as conscious willing, creates relationships. The more a person is alive and effective, the more she is aware of the possibility for relationships with other people; the more she lives, the more she realizes these relationships.

This is what we mean by community: it is the group of relationships created with other beings by the activity of personal consciousness and by the creative energy of personal will. The more I am aware and dynamic, the more I can create community, because I reach out and unite myself to an ever-greater number of beings. Community is like the halo of light from my personality; it is the field of my freedom in action; community is my I as it affirms itself. In a true sense, we can say that community is *me* in its greatest sense. Community is born from me; if I pull back, my community lessens.

And if we remember that in order to express herself, the person must communicate, must give—and that therefore the action of freedom is essentially love—we can clearly understand that community is the place where I *love*.

The conditions that the I finds in its actions are not suffered or tolerated like an enemy or a stranger with whom I make a pact or set limits; these are accepted, made my own, as if they were more from my own will: law becomes *freedom*.

The ideal of the community is no longer the equilibrium of justice, but the understanding and assimilation of love.

3.

Let us now apply to the phenomenon of communal prayer the observations made so far. To be concrete, we can give the example of the feast day Mass, the "Holy Day of Obligation." This can happen in two very different ways.

a. So I go to church for the festive Mass, in which a hundred other people participate. I enter interiorly isolated between the walls of my usual individualism and egotism, which makes me consider all the others with whom I am not linked by common interest or affective instinct indifferently or possibly in a hostile way. I am alone among strangers—a highly significant word, "strangers," that is, people who are outside of me, who have nothing to do with me. Those hundred people will weigh on me with their behavior dictated by different characteristics, or maybe they will distract me curiously, like *things* that happen before my eyes.

If I want to attend Mass well, all my strength must converge on isolating myself from these circumstances, on escaping these others as much as possible, on forgetting about them as if they were not there. In a similar case, the Christian assembly in the house of God would be, for me, a collectivity: the thanksgiving of this assembly would be, as such, only an obligation, a *law*: the event would be felt like a coercion of my spontaneous spirit, like a limit, like an anguish, which patience and devotion would succeed in tolerating.

The ideal in such a participation at Mass would be to remain as much as possible by myself.

b. Here is another case. I enter that church, among a hundred other people, unknown among strangers—people whom I have never seen before and whom I may never see again. Instinctively, I feel a sense of extraneousness, of confusion, of solitude. I *recollect* myself, I recollect the energies of my conscience, I recall who these people are for me, and I exclaim as my heart opens up: "God, I accept these people, all of them, because they are yours, they are mine, they are me, they are part of me; I pray for them. Our Father who art in Heaven. . . ."

The more mature my Christian personality is, the more profound, simple, and obvious this gesture of awareness, of gift, of *charity*, will be. In such a gesture, all the strength of my soul, instead of feeling constrained or restricted, is expanded. The presence of those people is embraced by the magnanimity of my Christian spirit—they become attached to me, almost integrated in my soul. That large presence opens up the strength of my voice, opens up the terms of my awareness, almost physically opens up my spirit. It builds me up, it exalts me—in the etymological sense of the word. My prayer is communitarian, and I experience how this expressive gesture in the presence of God is never as great as it is now.

Now, if these people were all distracted, and if they behaved unsuitably, then in order to accept them, I am obliged to an even greater awareness and a stronger dedication—that is, my gesture becomes more expressive, my personality is realized even more. Instead of being a *scandal*, instead of being a stumbling block on the path of my personality, this mass of people raises me up—that is, it assures that the dimensions of my spirit grow up in all of their space. And if instead it were a thousand, or ten thousand, so much more sublimely would I be exalted. The more they are, the more I am.

4.

What has been said about the festive Mass applies to the everyday actions of our liturgical life, to our singing or choral arrangements.

And the more such a spirit is understood and lived, the more the liturgical action or song or choir are shaped in beauty and in warmth—in *harmony*—even in their exterior result, in their material face.

Christ is the ideal of this lived communal dimension: because every one of his prayers embraced all of humanity in every time and space, Christ, the hero who runs the path of human existence. And it is wonderful to observe how the power of the communal will conquers every objection and every contradiction: Christ included in his gesture even his killers; forgiveness is the indicator of the supreme freedom of communal charity.

The cloister should be the place where above all this ideal aspect of Christ is imitated, where the charity of a conscious dedication to humanity is lived uninterruptedly, and where this charity is expressed in the gesture of a perennially communal prayer.

But the cloister in ecclesial life represents a paradigm and a calling to the loving and catholic space which should constitute the *dimension* of the daily life of every Christian, in its every small action, in whatever concrete situation we find ourselves.

Prayer: Memory of the Fact of Christ

1.

THE UNIQUE PROBLEM in life is the problem of faith: "My just one lives by faith."

The work that we do to recover the meaning of these words from the Bible is precisely in indicating how the main task of life is conversion—that is, *faith*. Faith is the recognition of the presence among us of another as the meaning of our life.

This implies a change in the consciousness of oneself, by which the personal subject is affirmed in my actions by affirming another, by *obeying* another. This change in self-awareness, in the concept of self, is the *metanoia* of the Gospel: conversion.

"I know nothing but Christ and Christ crucified"—*this* historical Christ, who happened like this. I know nothing but Christ, who reveals himself in these gestures, in these events. Therefore, while living "in the flesh," while in a dynamic of life that is phenomenologically human, I live another dynamic, "faith in the Son of God"; I live this new awareness of my being.

2.

Welcoming this—"recognizing" it in a deep sense, existentially, that which faith makes me see, to live by faith while living in the flesh—is charity, the relationship of love with Being.

All the logic of my actions must derive from this recognition; thus, all actions derive from the way in which everybody conceives of themselves, because our actions are nothing other than attempts to project into the relationships of time and space the awareness that we have of ourselves. Because of the changed awareness we have of ourselves, our actions tend to be produced in a different way.

From charity, which makes us recognize Christ, come actions whose law is charity.

3.

Now, because I live this new awareness of myself, I need there to be silence in me, from me. Interior silence is different from not talking, because consciousness must have a content, and therefore the problem is not just not speaking with the lips but the recognition of a new content of the self.

This new content of consciousness is, literally, the *memory* of him, of Christ.

Memory of him means memory of his gestures, because there does not exist a connection with a person except as a connection with his expression: it is in his expression that a person reveals himself, makes himself present.

The memory of him—that is, of his gestures ("do this in memory of me")—is the formula of silence. Silence is not just not talking, but turning toward something other, coming face to face with the gestures of Christ. Laurentius, a hermit, says: "It was said to me: everything must be welcomed without words and held in silence. So I realized that maybe my entire existence would be spent in understanding what had happened to me. And the memory of you filled the silence."

4.

"Do this in memory of me": what does the word "this" indicate? All his life is in that gesture, participates in that gesture, which is an efficacious cry for the salvation of the world and the glory of God—a saved humanity, a living humanity, is the glory of God.

Our life expresses itself fully like this; our life is life if it participates in that gesture.

We do not have anything higher to profess except a participation in that cry: in liturgical terms it is life as an *offering*.

"Father most holy and source of all holiness, sanctify these gifts. . . ." The bread and wine are the sign of our entire expression of life; therefore it is over us that the prayer is said; the bread is only the sign of the fact that we, in the totality of our life, become the body and blood of Christ, his body as a new creation.

5.

Our whole life is in this offering, this prayer, as the awareness of ourselves in so far as we belong to Christ. "We must pray ceaselessly": this is the word that indicates the authentic expression of our life's work.

Prayer is the proper content of life, and this is awareness, memory of the facts that happened, of the gestures of Christ and their consequences, their arrival within our history and our life. Therefore, the content of prayer is the *mirabilia Dei*, God's actions in our history, and among these the death and resurrection of Jesus as the fulcrum, the keystone.

The difference between prayer as the expression of natural religiosity and Christian prayer is that Christian prayer has a history as its content. Our whole life is summed up in that story.

6.

For this reason, if we do not want to reduce the yield of our involvement with Being and to go astray on our path, and if we do not want to feel our footsteps falter and lose our focus on the attraction of life, we should try to render our prayer adequately, formulating it along the lines of the prayers that have been left to us by the first and greatest among us: the *Magnificat* of Mary, the *Benedictus* of Zechariah, and the *Nunc dimittis* of Simeon.

Canticle of the Blessed Virgin Mary

My soul magnifies the Lord,
and my spirit rejoices in God my Savior,
for he has regarded the low estate of his handmaiden.
For behold, henceforth all generations
will call me blessed;
for he who is mighty has done great things for me,
and holy is his name.
And his mercy is on those who fear him
from generation to generation.

He has shown strength with his arm,
he has scattered the proud
in the imagination of their hearts,
he has put down the mighty from their thrones,
and exalted those of low degree;
he has filled the hungry with good things,
and the rich he has sent empty away.
He has helped his servant Israel,
in remembrance of his mercy,
as he spoke to our fathers,
to Abraham and to his posterity forever (Luke 1:46-55).

Canticle of Zechariah

Blessed be the Lord God of Israel,
for he has visited and redeemed his people,
and has raised up a horn of salvation for us
in the house of his servant David,
as he spoke by the mouth of his holy prophets from of old,
that we should be saved from our enemies,
and from the hand of all who hate us;
to perform the mercy promised
to our fathers,
and to remember his holy covenant,
the oath which he swore to our father Abraham,
to grant us that we, being delivered from the hand of our enemies,
might serve him without fear,
in holiness and righteousness
before him all the days of our life.
And you, child,
will be called the prophet of the Most High;
for you will go before the Lord
to prepare his ways,
to give knowledge of salvation to his people
in the forgiveness of their sins,
through the tender mercy of our God,
when the day shall dawn upon us from on high
to give light to those who sit in darkness
and in the shadow of death,
to guide our feet
into the way of peace (Luke 1:68-79).

Canticle of Simeon

Lord, now let thy servant depart in peace,
according to thy word;
for mine eyes have seen thy salvation
which thou hast prepared in the presence of all peoples,
a light for revelation to the Gentiles,
and for glory to thy people Israel (Luke 2: 29-32).

The structure of this prayer should become the structure of ours.

The liturgy is what educates us in this type of prayer: the liturgy, in fact, is entirely made up of *memory*.

7.

Every action is a prayer if it takes its direction, its structure, from the reality of one's gestures, from that memory, from liturgical prayer, which is the great paradigm.

Christ himself fixed the structure of the supreme expression of our personality, the supreme prayer as memory: the sacrament, of which Baptism is the beginning and the Eucharist is the end.

8.

If the supreme expression of prayer, and therefore of our person, is the sacrament, to live our life is to understand, to expound, the sacrament. This is the formula of our wisdom: to live every relationship as a sacrament. To live the sacrament is to live the salvation which has been given, which we already possess and to which we offer ourselves, in the concreteness of our relationships.

But we do not live the sacrament as a gesture—and much less as life—if in that gesture, and as a consequence in life, we are not dominated by the memory, that is, by the remembrance of his presence, which comes to us in time, the time of the cross and resurrection.

9.

Therefore the dominant feeling in the life of a Christian is to pray that this presence manifest himself. One does not love people and things, one does not love Christ, if everything in us does not aspire to realize itself in that "glory."

We already see this glory in its shy beginning. This is why in the Christian community the sacrament is really a *feast*, or in other words, joy.

In nothing else do the people of God feel themselves so ardently within something else, within a new world, as in the sacrament.

But if the sacrament is not rooted in life, if life is not a living of the sacrament, if all our actions do not tend toward expounding the sacrament, as the structure, as the dynamic of a sacramental paradigm, this novelty within existence, this pledge of eternity, will not claim our existence.

Holiness as Desire for Life

Saints Are Human

1.

THERE IS A certain image of holiness that represents the exceptionality of the saint with a halo. And yet being a saint is neither a profession for the few nor is it to become a museum piece. Holiness is the very fabric of Christian life.

Despite the inadequacy of certain images, a trace of the fundamental idea remains: the saint is not a superman; he is truly human. The saint is truly human because she adheres to God and therefore to the ideal for which her heart was made, of which her destiny is made. Ethically, all of this means "to do the will of God" within a humanity that remains human and yet somehow becomes different.

St. Paul testifies to the Galatians: "While living in the flesh, I live by faith in the Son of God." In fact, holiness is the reflection of the only one in whom humanity was fulfilled according to its full potentiality: Jesus Christ.

2.

Holiness is thus an active—vigilant—recognition of the fundamental need, of the ultimate realization of life's meaning, the *unum necessarium*, the "one thing necessary" of the Gospel.

The world seeks to reduce this fundamental need to the point of discouraging every expression of it, attempting to suffocate it; and this division is expressed in frantic volunteerism on the one hand and in psychoses on the other.

A relationship with God is the most adequate working hypothesis for the growth and realization of a unified personality. For this reason, the world still needs, today more than ever, the "spectacle of holiness," as Bardy describes the early days of Christianity, because the world needs the witness of unity, of the coherence of life with its fundamental need. St. Paul said: "We have become a spectacle to angels, to the world, and to ourselves" (cf. Gustave Bardy, *La conversion au christianisme durant les premiers siècles* [Aubier: Paris, 1949]).

3.

The most immediate aspect of this spectacle is the unity of consciousness that is created. To live the mystery of communion with God in Christ teaches us to see everything as related to a unique value wherein every judgment and every decision begin from a unique measure.

From this profound richness, there arises a vision of life lived with an amazing simplicity: a single, unique reality as the criterion and measure and way of seeing invests everything with its light, so that the I feels itself one with everything and in everything, even in front of death.

Ex uno verbo omnia, et unum loquuntur omnia, et hoc est principium quod et loquitur in vobis, says *The Imitation of Christ*: "From one word everything, and one thing speaks of everything, and this is the principle that speaks also in you."

Jacopone da Todi will proclaim the content of this word as it echoes in the human gaze and heart: "Love, love, the whole world shouts / love, love, everything shouts with it." This *everything*—in Latin *omne cosa*—identifies with detailed analysis the presence, in the one substance that cries out, of everything in its individuality, however great or small, while the "shouting with" reunites everything and involves everything in the symphony of a single meaning.

4.

A love of life, of God's creation—within a conscious and loyal embrace of its existential condition in the plan of God—characterizes the figure of the saint. In order to affirm his own life passionately, he has no need to forget or deny anything, much less, I will say, death.

In his essay *The Crisis of Civilization*, the great historian Huizinga noted: "Death is a part of the definition of life." Thus the eternal perspective gives the saint the ability to embrace death as a gesture of life, even in its "piercing pain," as Kierkegaard calls it in his *Diary*, and even while experiencing fear and anguish.

5.

What a difference between the hero of a purely rational ethics and the Christian saint! What a difference of true humanity—that is, of seriousness and understanding of human values, of realism and positive fruitfulness in front of the reality of death, the supreme test of humanity! Socrates is serene because "he will be freed" from the weight of the body; he flees a world that is conditioned and conditioning; St. Paul exclaims in the letter to the Christians of Corinth: "In reality, while we are in the body, we labor under a weight, not wanting to be stripped, but clothed over, so that what is mortal may be absorbed by life."

Death is redeemed; it is a passage to life.

There is nothing to pass over in silence, to avoid looking in the face, to escape artificially. It is precisely this impression of a forced, artificial dryness that one finds at heart in the imperturbability of the "Last Written Words" of Gaetano Salvemini, as reported in *Il Ponte*, September 1957. In contrast, a similar letter—the confession of the protagonist of *The Diary of a Country Priest* by Bernanos—makes the heart leap in front of all its human interest: "I, in front of death, will certainly not try to be either the hero or the stoic. And if I am afraid, I will say: I am afraid. But to Jesus Christ." And in this supreme test of humanity, we find again the true image: Jesus of Nazareth, who in front of death "began to be afraid and to feel anguish," as the Gospel narrates, and asks that death pass him by. But the strength of this just man makes him able to embrace the dreadful face of eternal goodness and meaning: "Still, not my will, but your will be done."

6.

The energy of the will is free of everything, a will no longer blocked and trapped in the violence of its own project but within the horizon of a true, eternal relationship. So the courage of a sacrifice to the point of total self-giving uses all the strength that comes from the reasonableness and limitless vitality of love.

The unity of our consciousness does not stop on the sidelines of a detached aestheticism but becomes operative and transformative, dominant in the entire space of the person and thus in time and space. The unity of the personality becomes a history of maturity that is both personal and for the other, for the world.

The Awareness of Incapacity

1.

A DEEP contradiction, like an original sickness, makes the human ideal exaggerated and difficult for every person, because intelligence and will remain existentially deprived of their ultimate energy and incapable of truly possessing their destiny: the saint is the person who most acutely and dramatically experiences this native fragility and this awareness of sin.

Being a sinner is the existential modality in which our ontological limits—which exist alongside our freedom—are most clearly documented. Truly, this instrument of the affirmation of our being, freedom, has an immanent limitation from which the possibility of evil, of sin, arises.

A mysterious original condition renders this possibility actual, by which we see that it is more surprising when we do not fail than when we fail. St. Francis de Sales will write: "Why are we surprised that weakness is weak?"

2.

In such a context, the overall attitude of the soul arising from our consciousness of self can only be humility. Virtue is a stable inclination toward the realization of a value, and it implies an ease in such realization: humility is this virtuous familiarity in conceiving ourselves within the total context, to feel that our very life is to be continually created, but more resoundingly, to recognize existence as a tireless getting up again.

One of the most beautiful liturgical prayers exclaims: "God, who above every changeable thing remains unchangeable, give strength to our heart; so that while we are tired out by what happens in time, we can always come back to your stability." The sense of this substantial fragility makes us hyper-sensitive to the possibility of evil in ourselves and to its actual presence penetrating the surface of our expressions: *Sine tuo numine, nihil est in homine, nihil est innoxium*: "without your creative force, there is nothing in man, nothing remains intact."

The saint lives this anthropological perception as a normal feeling. When St. Charles Borromeo brought along his confessor every time he traveled, in order to immerse himself every day in the sacrament of penance, he was not exaggerating; he lived the truth of his person.

3.

Humility rests on a deep calm, because the truth about ourselves leads to a peace that refreshes us, allows authentic life to flow again.

St. Paul's insistence on humility of heart is an invitation: "Rejoice, I say it again, rejoice."

But all of this is not a superficial and frantic tidying up of the labor of life, a sentimental obliteration of the complex and contradictory seriousness and drama of life. A humble calm can penetrate an active pain: the word mortification dominates in the life of the saint. A mortification that comes from the lived consciousness of one's own original impotence and total fragility: a substantial mortification of the I, the result of which is poverty of spirit.

Psychologically, such mortification is a condition of life: the poor one accepts the paradox with simplicity, and she loves the maturation of self that comes with renunciation, by which she recognizes salvation through the mysterious permission of evil.

The poor one knows that mortification is only an appearance, it is only "the semblance of death"—a fraught appearance, made concrete in struggle, strain, separation, pain—but in which one will find true life, "more life." God is not "God of the dead, but of the living," whose "glory" is "man fully alive," whose project is "mercy, not sacrifice." Because "the Son of Man did not come to condemn the world," but to free it.

Within the consciousness of our own evil and under the surface of our pain, the saint recognizes all of this with the simple heart of a child.

Affection for Christ

1.

ONLY THE companionship of the Son of God, which has penetrated into history and has gathered to its side "those whom the Father has given into his hands," gives man's life the capacity of fulfillment proportionate to his destiny: in the physiognomy of the saint, affection for Christ constitutes the most worthy and fascinating trait, and the sense of his presence, the most determining aspect.

In a certain sense, what the saint craves is not holiness in terms of perfection; it is holiness as encounter, attachment, adhesion, assimilation to Jesus Christ. The encounter with Christ gives the saint the certainty of a presence whose force frees her from evil and makes her freedom capable of doing good.

The figures of the great saints are often dominated by the importance that is given in their spiritual life to their strength of will. And it is true that they are impressive examples of this.

But all of that is just the obvious consequence of something else. The error may come from not understanding that the will of the saint is not the will to succeed, but it is a will for God, the active desire for another.

One can also stray from the Christian path through the wrong type of asceticism. In the presumption and claim to rely on factors that are supposedly more realistic, we forget that the only factor of our being in reality is the free power of God, the God who is able to give life to the dead, and, even more, "calls into existence the things that are from non-existence," as the mother of the Maccabees says in the Bible.

The power of God will transform my human confusion into a perfection according to his design, his justice.

2.

There is no ethical consequence that is more radical, more necessary, more absolute than this: the certainty of being transformed and therefore of being able to change. "He entrusted himself, hoping against hope," St. Paul says about Abraham.

This entrusting ourselves to another—hoping in him against the desperate appearance of our smallness, poverty, and fragility—is the first note of a present salvation; it is the beginning of the redemption that is making its fulfillment felt. *Spe salvi facti sumus*: "In hope we were saved."

And it is not the certainty in a salvation that comes after death, in the hereafter, but a certainty in a salvation that is already happening in my life: before I die, holiness penetrates me, justice possesses me. It is a certainty that challenges this time of misery, and the discomfort that the evidence of sin displays in me, because it finds its reason in the omnipotence of a reality in which I participate as a person, because it has chosen to give itself to me, to enter into the structure of my poverty: the power of Christ in me.

"The Father has given them into my hands"; "no one can take them out of my hands"—those who commend themselves to him, committing themselves in freedom, notwithstanding the contradictory stirring and the dramatic errors in their existence.

In her *Mistica oggettiva* (*Objective Mysticism*), Adrienne von Speyr observes: "Holiness does not consist in the fact that a man gives everything, but in the fact that the Lord takes everything"—in a certain sense even in spite of the one whom the Lord chooses. In fact, as von Speyr acutely testifies, "between offer and acceptance there is always a contrast, an error, an oversight. Man offers everything, maybe with his words, he pronounces the offering half-heartedly. Man imagines it always as something limited. His offering, notwithstanding his will, should not consider itself as nothing, nor as a figure conformed to this world. The Lord hears him as if he pronounced his offering in the correct way; and when he takes everything in this sense, then probably man shouts and regrets what has been taken, but the grace of holiness resides precisely in the fact that the Lord permits this oversight."

3.

Following Jesus Christ implies a real poverty from the psychological and ethical point of view.

St. Paul shows us a paradigm for this poverty of spirit in the Letter to the Philippians when, speaking of Jesus Christ, he says that the Lord "being God did not hold on to his being God," but in a certain sense renounced his divinity, to become like us, "assuming the form of a slave." Of him, Paul says that "he annihilated himself": *exinanivit*.

In the spiritual life of the Christian, this poverty reverberates psychologically in an analogous experience of our nothingness, of our own powerlessness, of a total poverty of self, but precisely as the consequence of the content of an ethical directive, which is abandonment to Christ.

The moral theme does not mean the stripping of the self, except as the result of the search for Christ, or better yet, the imitation of Christ: it has to do with recognizing this value, of letting ourselves be invaded by the choice of that which has value; in its depth, it has to do with making a judgment of recognition and of welcoming this vibrant and moving content into the materiality of one's own existence.

Thus, Christian renunciation is not the object of a choice, the result of our choice. The saint in the truest sense does not renounce something for Christ but desires Christ, desires the event of Christ in such a way that his life is permeated by him, even visually, as the form of his life: renunciation is just the appearance of this permeation.

The mystery of Christ has "identified us" with him, as the Letter to the Ephesians says; it has taken us into itself and therefore lives in the depths of our being like a new seed, like a new structure, that acts on our existence, transforming it according to the time and the way that the Father foresees, toward a perfect assimilation.

Therefore, the mystery of Christ is that event—by its nature perennially new—which should constitute the exhaustive object of consideration for the spiritual life, from which a complete hope springs: the complete hope that is the only thing capable of effectively liberating the energy of the I for the action of justice, for the *opus Dei*: "the work of God."

4.

The character of liberation forms the I in a radically new attitude, first of all toward itself: in the surprising novelty that springs up in us, like *aqua saliens in vitam aeternam*, like "water springing up to everlasting life," we begin to understand, to accept, to bear ourselves; we forgive ourselves.

In other words: if we give priority to this something new that we are, in so far as we abandon ourselves to the redemptive and transformative event of Christ, then we are able to recover ourselves, to embrace ourselves *fraternally*, in whatever condition.

If instead the point of view is first of all our success, our capacity for a particular outcome, then we lose ourselves: with the same violence that we affirm our pride and passion, we irresistibly awaken delusion; from the same weight of attachment to ourselves, from self-love we are dragged down into self-recrimination and disgust with ourselves, no longer having a joyful perspective, despairing of any continuity, destroying every consistency, breaking down any tenacity, and in the end suffocating ourselves.

The worldly ideal is success and the worldly project is an attitude with which one fights with all seriousness to have success, with one's power of foresight, with one's calculation and dispensation of energies and means.

5.

The Christian's worth resides in the project of God for our life: we recognize and accept it as our own structure and story.

And such a story implies a presence in and around us in which all the richness of the destiny of our person can come true. Through this presence, we know ourselves already as new creatures: "If anyone is in Christ, there is a new creation: everything old has passed away; see, everything has become new!" Paul will say to the Christians at Corinth.

Christians are sure of the new and eternal covenant within us; therefore we will triumph, in ourselves and in the world: "This is the victory that overcomes the world, our faith," John affirmed. And the reason we will triumph is that "God is faithful to his promise."

6.

The ways in which victory comes for the Christian, though, can never be contained in the imagination. If our richness is in the gesture with which God comes, we cannot foresee the way and the time of his affirming himself, of his bringing fulfillment to our life.

Thus our salvation, our perfection, already exists, but at the same time it still has to manifest itself. It is as if we must always have our ears open, awaiting a new coming, or a return: the return of Christ.

In no way—we repeat it—is the Christian attitude determined toward an object which he formulates: the qualifying object is the "coming of Christ." Our attitude is one of waiting, waiting for Christ to come within us—and through us into the world—in holiness. Christians await and desire to be purified from all our sins, but no sin could ever negate our expectation.

So we desire the coming of Christ in us—and through us into the world—more than being attached to our sins or dominated by them. This expectation will bear fruit in God's time: "Whoever meditates on the law of God day and night will bear fruit in his time." The time of God, that is.

This is the radical abolition of moralism, because Christian morality is the story of God in man. Our freedom is not so much in what we manage to accomplish, because this depends on God: it is rather in the truth with which we seek God, in the truth with which we beg for Christ.

This is the essential decision in which freedom happens: seeking the truth. It is the attitude that permits a continuity without end: "Pray always" is Christ's invitation.

7.

Living in this attitude, the evil that is always in our life becomes more and more, as a criterion, an isolated fact; it is no longer able to *conquer* as an accepted perspective, no longer established as a program.

If we say: "Lord, hurry up and change me" or "Lord, take this sin from me," we cry out to the Lord because we are anticipating the Lord's manifestation.

But if we say: "I am deciding that my action will no longer be like this," how can we be Christian, if we have not lived the consciousness of the fact that under the form of his apparent energy there is another form of strength that sustains us, as an always unmerited gift, as *grace*?

In front of the limit of our evil, the prevailing desire of the Christian cannot be to act with our own strength to root it out: our own strength would obviously have the same weak will that committed the evil. The prevailing desire should be for something that is underneath all the limits and weaknesses, in which these things find nourishment, something which is able to undermine all that, which works in us at a deeper level than that to which our attachment to passions clings.

The prevailing desire in the Christian should be the return of Christ, Christ's manifestation in our own personality, in our own gestures, in our whole existence. The mystery, Christ, which is situated in our flesh and in our spirit through Baptism, Penance, and Eucharist, is made visible in the living expression of our I, as one of the beautiful prayers of the Lenten liturgy says: "O God . . . grant that we may manifest in our works the hidden reality of this sacrament." All our sins, chased out by the constancy of such a desire, will find themselves continually in a situation that is more and more fleeting, ephemeral.

In poverty of spirit, as the Christian tradition calls it, the regenerative and refreshing root of this desire, we begin to become Christian, to become saints, true persons: "Liberated from every evil," as a monastic hymn from Lenten Vespers begins: here (it is good to repeat it) is the first sign, the first reverberation and glow of the experience of that redemption which is Christ communicated to our being, the mysterious seed of a new existence. The invocation that we make to the Father in assuming our miserable condition—"Deliver us from evil"—and which the liturgy repeats as a humble and passionate echo—"Deliver us from every evil"—finds its first fulfillment in the desire for him to manifest himself in us, victorious over our human measure.

That such a desire should become the capacity of our heart, the supreme content of our values, the acutely privileged object of our will, beneath all our misery—this is a miracle, the miracle of holiness. "The thought of the love shown us in Christ"—St. Paul says to the Christians of Corinth—"impels us with the thought that if one died for all, all died . . . so that all those who live may live no longer for themselves but for him who died and rose for them."

8.

The expectation of Christ's final return—lived not as the resolution of present anguish or a formula for detachment, or even recrimination of the present time, but as the urgency to be awake to the truth of every contingent commitment, as the prophetic content of every serious love and responsibility toward the concrete path of life, even in the smallest details—constitutes the most disconcerting surprise provoked by this new humanity in the eyes of the world; and it is the most admirable spectacle and the most challenging sign for those who come across it and react with human sensibility and reflect with seriousness of spirit, while in the quiet astonishment of their heart they do not understand how this can happen.

9.

In this expectation, a surprising affection for Christ flourishes, which is the supreme gift of the Spirit and the most authentic miracle of the Christian life, of holiness.

Whoever is able to stutter the first words and make the first hesitant, fragile steps does not feel peculiar but already perceives herself in concert with the burning love of certain saints, with the tenacious tenderness operative in them.

The paradox of Paul shines clearly: "I am overcome with joy in my tribulation." But what more acute tribulation is there than our own imperfections and errors! So also, the determining presence is the love with which Christ gave himself to us and the affection generated by the attachment and abandonment of ourselves to him: thus the paradox of a humble, secure joy lives in that tribulation because he is already victorious, and "we have this firm hope, that he who has begun this good work in us will bring it to fulfillment on that day," as Paul testifies to the Christians of Philippi.

In the beautiful spiritual drama written by Oscar Milosz, entitled *Miguel Manara*, Gironima, the pure, feminine protagonist, says to her friend: "You seem a bit surprised to see me so happy. Do not begrudge me this tranquility of spirit and of heart: I do not neglect any of my duties." The privilege given to one who abandons everything to Christ, the determining presence of my own I and the maker of my destiny, does not obliterate and does not sidestep the intelligent, serious engagement that makes judgments, the reason that searches, or the heart that is committed to the point of sacrificing itself, or the will that spends its energy in the tension of a struggle or a daily work: this privilege allows all of this to come true and to *endure* in time. The abandonment of the self to Christ implies the co-involvement of all the forces of the I.

What we want to affirm, characterizing the Christian life or holiness, is that everything is done for a love. The dynamic of life is a working *for* someone. The unique meaning of life is that of being a gift. This is the great law, the great ethical value of which Christ spoke to us, and which the cross demonstrated. Life should be animated by the desire for dedication, by an impossibility to conceive of time and of ourselves—which is the essential content of life—other than as the tireless working for, within, a love.

And this dedication lives in the mortification of the self as the center and project of action. The saint understands all of this from the clarity with which Christ, in his flesh, described existence as suffering.

So for the saint Christ is the immediate object of his eyes and his heart.

Part of a People

1.

SAINT PAUL AFFIRMED to the Christians of Corinth: "Christ exists before all things and all things have consistency in him." Christ is the consistency of the saint.

Nothing expresses better the psychology of the saint's self-awareness than what St. Paul says: "I live: not I; it is Christ who lives in me." Christ becomes the truest content of my sense of self. Christ supplies and sustains the impotence of man's energy, as St. Paul experienced: "I can do all things in him who is my strength."

Therefore, the true meaning of the saint in the original Christian tradition is the one who recognizes "the coming in the flesh" of the Son of God, the one who has become involved in the new and eternal covenant and lives in responsibility, *responding* to this.

In fact, it is within this conscious friendship—this existential involvement with the presence, the company of God—that we acquire a new personality: the personality being determined by the ultimate meaning which the I recognizes and from the tension lived in pursuing it; it is a new theme of life, and a powerful yearning following from this, that defines the face of the Christian: "And whoever has this hope purifies himself as he is pure," St. John told the first Christians.

The ideal of such a dynamic is, as the Lord said: "Be perfect as your heavenly Father is perfect," but its concrete mode is in paying attention to a living presence: "Follow me."

The new and eternal covenant is the place of conversion, an environment that becomes the inexhaustible source of the flow of life as ascesis, as "work": "My Father is continually at work, and so I am at work." The companionship of Christ becomes the environment of a true morality, of time as an undaunted tension toward the fulfillment of the self.

St. Paul will describe this moral figure with dramatic suggestiveness in the third chapter of his letter to the Christians of Philippi: "Not that I have already reached the end or am already perfect; but I stretch out for it, to conquer it, because I myself have already been conquered by Christ." St. Ambrose seems to echo this authentic ethic, confirming it in Christian history, when he writes: "Holiness is not making no mistakes, but continually seeking not to fall."

Holiness is born then from a judgment of unity, from the perception and recognition of the I completely within the "cosmos" of God and within his story, which is Christ.

2.

Holiness thus becomes an experience of a radically new culture. A new perception of self, of humanity, of things, of events is enkindled and takes place in the relationship with the mystery of Christ, and this perception tends, in either an implicit or a conscious way, but always passionately, to a critical, systematic, organic conception of reality.

The exegesis of Fr. Huby notes the radical conversion of St. Paul's intellectual life in this way: "In [Christ] everything was created as a center of unity, of harmony, of cohesion, that gives the world its significance, its value, and through this, its reality, or to use another metaphor, as the place where all the threads, all the generators of the universe, link up and coordinate. Whoever establishes a point of view on the whole universe, past, present, and future, sees every being suspended ontologically in Christ and becoming definitively intelligible through him. . . . Fixed in him, everything is kept, so to speak, together. . . . The Christ is their principle of cohesion and harmony; he makes of the created world a *cosmos*, an ordered universe. . . . He is therefore the dominating center and the key of the universe."

We can call the cultural event that flows from this new point of view the culture of the "already happened": the fulfillment, the way, the truth, and the life, the meaning and the perfection that we seek, are already among us and within us; every action is an irresistible and immense manifestation of him. Truth, beauty, and justice are the blueprint of the real human being who lives by faith: "The glory of God is man fully alive."

3.

Therefore, holiness, as the origin of culture, is something that organizes a people, a new people: the ideal of the building of a people is the fullest dimension of an authentic culture and of holiness.

The holiness of God, involving itself in the old covenant with Abraham, generated a people. "You will be for me a kingdom of priests and a holy nation."

A kingdom of priests: a people made up of those who exercise an intermediary function between reality and God, a people whose profession of life is to affirm the relationship with God as constitutive of all human and cosmic realities.

A holy nation: in the nomenclature of natural religion, the holy is often associated with the words segregated, precious, consecrated in a special way. Thus God is holy because he is over every earthly thing. The holy is something dedicated only to God and not to the things of this world. Thus that nation is holy because it should "have no other God but the Lord": it should not recognize any other meaning for reality than the Lord nor find any source for living than in the voice that indicates his design.

Therefore, these people will not get mixed up with what the Bible calls the "abominations of the nations," which refer to idolatrous and magical practices: they must not abandon themselves to any actions that consign humanity to images of powers and therefore to conceptions of the world that in reality do not truly possess us and so cannot save us. "Hear, Israel: the Lord is our God, the Lord alone," Deuteronomy will warn.

In the old covenant, the saint was the one who belonged to such a people, who participated in such a mentality, in such a "measure" of the real. The difference with the nations was not only ethnic: it was more profoundly spiritual and thus more culturally explicit.

For this reason, in the original Christian tradition, the true meaning of the world "saint" is the one who recognizes, as we have already noted, "the coming in the flesh" of the Son of God. Throughout the flow of history, the saint is the one who has been called to recognize, and in fact to live, the mystery of Christ "in his body which is the Church," according to the Pauline phrase.

4.

In this comprehensive and vast sense, every Christian belongs to the "communion of saints," wherever her life does not disown its substance.

The Church appears as the miraculous place where true humanity, according to the design of God, comes within the reach of everyone. The life of the Church is the true treasure hidden, to purchase which is worth selling everything. The Church appears always more, along the path of her existence, as the environment in which morality becomes possible, as a daily effort more than as a particular outcome.

Our daily life remains invested and exalted by this design. In *The Tidings Brought to Mary*, which is the most beautiful song about Christian holiness in our times, Paul Claudel makes Pierre de Craon say: "Holiness does not mean to kiss a leper on the mouth or to die in pagan territory, but to do the will of God, promptly, whether it means staying where you are or going higher up."

The foundation is Christ; the fullness is already fulfilled. The work of each person is to be converted to this. One can build on this foundation in many ways, and the work of each one will reveal its value; we each put ourselves into this building as we can, even if the judgment of God burns up what we built up with straw and hay.

Our fullness is found—is realistically imagined and reached—in view of that judgment that will come to measure how we have been integrated within the construction. The Christian dynamic is located here: it is good to be a living stone in the building. The morality of our work is given by a precise criterion: the building of the body of Christ.

5.

The Christian path revolutionizes the moralities that we have constructed for ourselves. Every ethical theory ultimately says that the problem is to do good and avoid evil, but the real problem is: what constitutes the true good?

The good, for the Christian, consists in building the body of Christ. For this reason, we can affirm that the path of holiness for the Christian is the edification of the Church.

The positive content of life lies in being continually moved by this, in re-assuming such a motive as the life of one's own life. Let us say it again: the value is not measured by results. And this frees the person, in the abandonment to "God who justifies," and makes one paradoxically more capable of a result.

In the spontaneous surge of youthful life, as also in the lucid calm of maturity, the supreme commandment of Christ—"love God with your whole being" and "love your neighbor as yourself" —is made concrete in that living, active availability of total dedication to the mystery of the Church, which animates every project, but also judges the value and the feeling of every action.

Again, Claudel lends to these experiences the dramatic voice of symbolism when he has the father of Violaine, Anne Vercors, exclaim before the body of his dead daughter: "What is the world worth compared to a life? And what is life for if not to be given away? And why do we torment ourselves when it is so much easier to obey?"

6.

Holiness in the Church is not just an exceptional fact. The canonized saints—saints in the restricted sense of the word—are the figures that God has established to reveal a particular role, as witnesses in the history of the people of God, and to become a pedagogical paradigm for a mature relationship with the Mystery that is for all those who are called: "The saints are the demonstration of the possibility of Christianity, therefore they can be guides on the road toward the love of God which would otherwise seem impossible," von Speyr says.

In the physiognomy and in the path of the saints, the Christian beholds, as if on a big screen, the structure of our own figures which are still embryonic and the traits of our own path which is still short and undeveloped.

Therefore, in the beginnings of the Christian event, even in the fervor of the beginning, the *Didache* recommended: "Seek the faces of the saints every day, and take comfort in their words."

Conclusion

The Christian announcement is the announcement of the new humanity we are called to become and, in taking on this new humanity, to change the world.

This has already begun to change and will change everything when God desires, when the story of Christ will be fulfilled.

We cannot present ourselves to the world—and to ourselves in the measure we share the situation of our world—except by starting from this content: the content of holiness in the new and eternal covenant. This is the weight, the responsibility, that we have in our hands: not immediately our virtue, our solidarity, not our structures, our institutions, not our ideals or our moral feelings, but the announcement of something that has happened.

The true problem of Christian holiness is not the choice of an attitude to have in the world but the recognition of something which has happened and is given to us and which changes our attitude, our face, every day.

We find our value in the objective reality of this happening, to which we adhere, by which we let ourselves be penetrated. The key is not in leaning on ourselves but adhering to something that "has appeared in the flesh." "Do this in memory of me."

The Sense of Sin

The Roots of Sin and the Definitions of Sin

1.

WHEN JESUS SAYS in the Gospel: "When the Son of man comes, will he find faith on earth?" he was speaking not only to the audience present there, for those who had openly refused his word, but he was saying it to the apostles, in front of his disciples. We Christians are the first ones who are obliged to recognize that the fundamental problem of our existence is indicated by one little word: faith.

The particular usage of this word that will be decisive for our meditation on the roots of sin is indicated by this passage from the Letter to the Galatians:

> We ourselves, who are Jews by birth and not Gentile sinners, yet who know that a man is not justified by works of the law but through faith in Jesus Christ, even we have believed in Christ Jesus, in order to be justified by faith in Christ, and not by works of the law, because by works of the law shall no one be justified. But if, in our endeavor to be justified in Christ, we ourselves were found to be sinners, is Christ then an agent of sin? Certainly not! But if I build up again those things which I tore down, then I prove myself a transgressor. For I through the law died to the law, that I might live to God. I have been crucified with Christ; it is no longer I who live, but Christ who lives in me; and the life I now live in the flesh I live by faith in the Son of God, who loved me and gave himself for me. I do not nullify the grace of God; for if justification were through the law, then Christ died to no purpose (Galatians 2:15-21).

Where does our personal hope for salvation find support?

Our answer is important, because the depth of hope, which for the majority of life may remain unconscious, sustains our human existence, generates that energy, the tension that allows us to live.

This passage from the Letter to the Galatians makes precise references, which the exegetes illustrate; it makes concrete links with the Jewish law and in a particular way with the law of circumcision.

The analogy we make to our own life is not only licit, but imperative. The dialectic between law (circumcision) and Christ who saves is really the same dialectic between our works—even those taken up in the name of God and of the Church, the dialectic between our intelligence and will in action—and something that comes much before this, something that is not ours, even if, as Paul says at the end of this passage, it is given to us. It is nearly impossible to avoid the accusation that we tend to put our hope in our own activity.

In our normal activity, we unconsciously put our hope in our works and not in the fact of Christ; we do not judge and do not experience how, in the concrete, he saves us.

The answer to that question is important because the consistency of our personality lies in the place where we put our hope, lies in the content of our hope, because the ultimate consistency of life is oriented toward the future: from the future we borrow our reason for living, or better, it is in the future that we want to discover the answer to the questions life asks.

Where, then, is our hope?

I wanted to underline this passage from the Letter to the Galatians to establish a point of view that, in my opinion, reveals the meaning of conversion. Conversion is the path from hope in our own power to hope in the fact of the living Christ, of Christ who lives in me, where "the life I now live in the flesh I live by faith in the Son of God."

Here is the authoritative and radical observation that the passage from Paul proposes. Even *our* work—the engagement of our own will as the transformative subject of our moral life—is not immune from what we have called hope in our own activity. Thus, it sometimes seems right to place our hope in our moral purity, while even this supreme value of human activity has to be taken up entirely by the fact of Christ.

We should take those words of Paul—"the love of Christ"—not as a figure of speech but as the only fact capable of giving us consistency. The Pauline expression establishes with incredible energy the physiognomy of the new humanity, of the new creature and the new creation, as St. Peter will say.

When we put our hope in our moral life, we do not realize how grotesque our attitude becomes. Holiness itself must not be understood as the fruit of our activity but as a gift, actively—certainly—sought and desired from the fact of Christ. This does not take anything away from the moral law, not one iota: "For I through the law died to the law"; but, in order to have a real and pure moral strength, I do not trust in my moral will; my hope is not in my activity, in my moral effort, but in his grace, that is, in his presence lovingly active in me.

It is in front of the fact of Christ that the recognition of ourselves as sinners becomes realistic and fruitful. At the beginning of the Eucharistic liturgy, the Church's most important gesture, the Church asks us to have a penitential attitude. And because the possibility for a relationship of communion with others is modeled on the fact of the Eucharist, our relationships would be true if only they *started* from the awareness of our sinfulness. "If we say we have no sin, we deceive ourselves, and the truth is not in us. If we confess our sins, he is faithful and just, and will forgive our sins and cleanse us from all unrighteousness. If we say we have not sinned, we make him a liar, and his word is not in us" (1 John 1:8-10).

We recall this point again in the First Letter of St. John, when he speaks about the unity that comes from communion.

"We are writing this to you, that which we have seen and heard we proclaim also to you, so that you may have communion with us; and we are writing this that our joy may be complete. God is light, this is the message we have heard from him: if we say we have communion with him while we walk in darkness, we lie and do not live according to the truth."

The "darkness" is everything that does not accord with the fact of Christ. The roots of sin, then, are in wanting to turn to something else as the source of our hope, something else to inspire our action.

Let us reflect on this powerful image from Jeremiah:

> At that time, says the Lord, the bones of the kings of Judah, the bones of its princes, the bones of the priests, the bones of the prophets, and the bones of the inhabitants of Jerusalem shall be brought out of their tombs; and they shall be spread before the sun and the moon and all the host of heaven, which they have loved and served, which they have gone after, and which they have sought and worshiped; and they shall not be gathered or buried; they shall be as dung on the surface of the ground. Death shall be

preferred to life by all the remnant that remains of this evil family in all the places where I have driven them, says the Lord of hosts.

You shall say to them, Thus says the Lord:
When men fall, do they not rise again?
    If one turns away, does he not return?
Why then has this people turned away
    in perpetual backsliding?
They hold fast to deceit,
    they refuse to return.
I have given heed and listened,
    but they have not spoken aright;
no man repents of his wickedness,
    saying, "What have I done?"
Everyone turns to his own course,
    like a horse plunging headlong into battle.
Even the stork in the heavens
    knows her times;
and the turtledove, swallow, and crane
    keep the time of their coming;
but my people know not
    the ordinance of the Lord.
How can you say, "We are wise,
    and the law of the Lord is with us"?
But behold, the false pen of the scribes
    has made it into a lie.
The wise men shall be put to shame,
    they shall be dismayed and taken;
lo, they have rejected the word of the Lord,
    and what wisdom is in them?
Therefore I will give their wives to others
    and their fields to conquerors,
because from the least to the greatest
    everyone is greedy for unjust gain;
from prophet to priest
    everyone deals falsely.
They have healed the wound of my people lightly,
    saying, "Peace, peace,"
when there is no peace.
Were they ashamed when they committed abomination?
    No, they were not at all ashamed;
    they did not know how to blush.
Therefore they shall fall among the fallen;
    when I punish them, they shall be overthrown,

says the Lord.
When I would gather them, says the Lord,
there are no grapes on the vine,
nor figs on the fig tree;
even the leaves are withered,
and what I gave them has passed away from them
(Jeremiah 8:1-13)

We have forgotten the law of God, which is a fact in history; we have forgotten the faith and have substituted our moralism instead—moral preaching, something that any wise or prudent man of the world might preach. We have directed our energies toward a hope based on our strength of will and attempt to measure the dignity of our actions by our own power.

The fact of Christ, and not our own works, is the point of reference.

We can now understand how our method of relating with ourselves and with others can change radically.

2.

We should continually repeat to ourselves what it means to sin: according to the Bible first, and not according to moral philosophy.

First of all, sin is a lack of fidelity to the fact of God—not to the fact that God exists, but to that fact with which God has entered our life, a lack of fidelity to the God who has made himself a fact in our life.

Here are two passages from the Bible that help us understand this:

Remember the days of old,
consider the years of many generations;
ask your father, and he will show you;
your elders, and they will tell you.
When the Most High gave to the nations their inheritance,
when he separated the sons of men,
he fixed the bounds of the peoples
according to the number of the sons of God.
For the Lord's portion is his people,
Jacob his allotted heritage.
He found him in a desert land,
and in the howling waste of the wilderness;
he encircled him, he cared for him,
he kept him as the apple of his eye.
Like an eagle that stirs up its nest,

that flutters over its young,
spreading out its wings, catching them,
bearing them on its pinions,
the Lord alone did lead him,
and there was no foreign god with him.
He made him ride on the high places of the earth,
and he ate the produce of the field;
and he made him suck honey out of the rock,
and oil out of the flinty rock.
Curds from the herd, and milk from the flock,
with fat of lambs and rams,
herds of Bashan and goats,
with the finest of the wheat—
and of the blood of the grape you drank wine.
But Jesh'urun waxed fat, and kicked;
you waxed fat, you grew thick, you became sleek;
then he forsook God who made him
and scoffed at the Rock of his salvation.
They stirred him to jealousy with strange gods;
with abominable practices they provoked him to anger.
They sacrificed to demons which were no gods,
to gods they had never known,
to new gods that had come in of late,
whom your fathers had never dreaded.
You were unmindful of the Rock that begot you,
and you forgot the God who gave you birth
(Deuteronomy 32:7-18).

Let me sing for my beloved
a love song concerning his vineyard:
My beloved had a vineyard
on a very fertile hill.
He digged it and cleared it of stones,
and planted it with choice vines;
he built a watchtower in the midst of it,
and hewed out a wine vat in it;
and he looked for it to yield grapes,
but it yielded wild grapes.
And now, O inhabitants of Jerusalem
and men of Judah,
judge, I pray you, between me
and my vineyard.
What more was there to do for my vineyard,

that I have not done in it?
When I looked for it to yield grapes,
why did it yield wild grapes?
And now I will tell you
what I will do to my vineyard.
I will remove its hedge,
and it shall be devoured;
I will break down its wall,
and it shall be trampled down.
I will make it a waste;
it shall not be pruned or hoed,
and briers and thorns shall grow up;
I will also command the clouds
that they rain no rain upon it.
For the vineyard of the Lord of hosts
is the house of Israel,
and the men of Judah
are his pleasant planting;
and he looked for justice,
but behold, bloodshed;
for righteousness,
but behold, a cry!
Woe to those who join house to house,
who add field to field,
until there is no more room,
and you are made to dwell alone
in the midst of the land.
The Lord of hosts has sworn in my hearing:
Surely many houses shall be desolate,
large and beautiful houses, without inhabitant (Isaiah 5:1-9).

According to another biblical image, sin is *forgetfulness* of God. Our lack of fidelity has an effect: the fact of God does not determine life. Forgetfulness is the root of infidelity, a tremendous distraction whose consequence is a man who is torn, dissolved, distracted from his end, tossed about here and there.

The word of the Lord came to me, saying, "Go and proclaim in the hearing of Jerusalem, Thus says the Lord:

I remember the devotion of your youth,
your love as a bride,
how you followed me in the wilderness,
in a land not sown.

Israel was holy to the Lord,
the first fruits of his harvest.
All who ate of it became guilty;
evil came upon them,
says the Lord.

Hear the word of the Lord, O house of Jacob, and all the families of the house of Israel. Thus says the Lord:

What wrong did your fathers find in me
that they went far from me,
and went after worthlessness, and became worthless?
They did not say, "Where is the Lord
who brought us up from the land of Egypt,
who led us in the wilderness,
in a land of deserts and pits,
in a land of drought and deep darkness,
in a land that none passes through,
where no man dwells?"
And I brought you into a plentiful land
to enjoy its fruits and its good things.
But when you came in you defiled my land,
and made my heritage an abomination.
The priests did not say, "Where is the Lord?"
Those who handle the law did not know me;
the rulers transgressed against me;
the prophets prophesied by Ba'al,
and went after things that do not profit.
Therefore I still contend with you,
says the Lord,
and with your children's children I will contend.
For cross to the coasts of Cyprus and see,
or send to Kedar and examine with care;
see if there has been such a thing.
Has a nation changed its gods,
even though they are no gods?
But my people have changed their glory
for that which does not profit.
Be appalled, O heavens, at this,
be shocked, be utterly desolate,
says the Lord,
for my people have committed two evils:
they have forsaken me,
the fountain of living waters,

and hewed out cisterns for themselves,
broken cisterns,
that can hold no water.
Is Israel a slave? Is he a homeborn servant?
Why then has he become a prey?
The lions have roared against him,
they have roared loudly.
They have made his land a waste;
his cities are in ruins, without inhabitant.
Moreover, the men of Memphis and Tah'panhes
have broken the crown of your head.
Have you not brought this upon yourself
by forsaking the Lord your God,
when he led you in the way?
And now what do you gain by going to Egypt,
to drink the waters of the Nile?
Or what do you gain by going to Assyria,
to drink the waters of the Euphra'tes?
Your wickedness will chasten you,
and your apostasy will reprove you.
Know and see that it is evil and bitter
for you to forsake the Lord your God;
the fear of me is not in you,
says the Lord God of hosts (Jeremiah 2:1-19).

Insofar as our life is not invested and determined by his presence, a presence which became a fact in history and in our life, our life remains distracted and empty.

We are actually used to affirming the totality of God's value as a theoretical affirmation, as an abstract affirmation about existence. God is not perceived, recognized in our life according to the totality of determination that he should have for us.

We seem not to realize that he is not the God of the dead, the God of our analyses, of our conceptions, but the God of the living, the God who became a fact in our history, who made *us* come out of Egypt, who freed *us* from slavery, who gave Jesus Christ for *us*.

I believe that sin, from which come old age and death, consists in not accepting that everything happens through God, who became a fact in history—that everything exists in service to our life in Christ.

And this is, in reality, how we reject him. Like a mother who accepts that she is having a child but does not accept that this child within her will make her belly grow or her legs swell—this is man, who recognizes God and Christ, but runs away from the labor and difficulty of forming and determining all of his undertakings "in His Name."

The Bible gives two other definitions of sin.

One is in the third chapter of the Gospel of John: *to refuse the light.* The word "light" as St. John uses it is much more pregnant than the metaphor of light that we have nowadays. Light is what makes things true, what makes it possible to see things in their reality: it is the truth of things.

The second comes from the words of the prophet Jeremiah and explains sin as *not listening to the word of God.*

Even here let us remember that the expression "word of God," according to the biblical mentality, is something that penetrates existence, because through this word God gives identity to Israel and engages with his people.

Thus, to lose the word of God is to lose ourselves, as Isaiah also says; and Jesus reminds us of this in a terrible way in the Gospel: "If salt loses its flavor, what is it worth anymore?"

In conclusion, this passage from Jeremiah can help us illuminate these ideas:

> Thus says the Lord of hosts, the God of Israel: "Add your burnt offerings to your sacrifices, and eat the flesh. For in the day that I brought them out of the land of Egypt, I did not speak to your fathers or command them concerning burnt offerings and sacrifices. But this command I gave them, 'Obey my voice, and I will be your God, and you shall be my people; and walk in all the way that I command you, that it may be well with you.' But they did not obey or incline their ear, but walked in their own counsels and the stubbornness of their evil hearts, and went backward and not forward. From the day that your fathers came out of the land of Egypt to this day, I have persistently sent all my servants the prophets to them, day after day" (Jeremiah 7:21-25).

The Dynamic of Sin

1.

WHAT ARE the commandments, the laws, the judgments of the Lord? They are a directive that springs from a fact in which we are involved, an indication born from our intimacy with God—not an imaginary intimacy (built on the strength of our invention) but an intimacy to which God has objectively called us, touching our lives in an existential way.

The commandments and the law, according to their biblical value, do not rest on our concept of duty, on our formulation of duty; they come instead from a power in which we participate.

A child that is with her mother is able to not be afraid in front of a difficulty because she is *together*, because she is involved in a relationship. If the mother says: "My child, go up that mountain," the child would not know how to do it: this is how the command looks in the moralistic understanding of the law. Instead, with mom or dad, *in company*, the child can be fearless in front of a daunting path. The judgments, the laws of the Lord, are the Lord who intervenes in my life, calling me to be part of the history of his people: the Lord who puts me with others and from whom a new dynamic of behavior bursts forth.

Sin is to go against this fact of God, to refuse to be involved with him, to forget what God has done for us. Conversely, the individualistic position can easily cause me to despair, by putting me in front of sin in moralistic terms: "I have to, because I should be able to do this."

I have touched on these biblical terms of law, command, judgment. God's commands, his laws, make us capable, give us a power that we have *in so far as we are close to him*, close as a child is to her mother and to her father, like a child who feels at home.

The home is a fact, not a list of laws. It does not have to do with moral ideals except as they are connected to an awareness of the fact in which we are caught up. We remember that when Scripture speaks of life's dynamism, it uses this fundamental expression "in the name of the Lord"—that is, owing to the power with which he reaches our lives and the work that he is doing in us.

The Lord says in Leviticus (11:44-45): "For I am the Lord your God; consecrate yourselves therefore, and be holy, for I am holy. You shall not defile yourselves with any swarming thing that crawls upon the earth. For I am the Lord who brought you up out of the land of Egypt, to be your God; you shall therefore be holy, for I am holy."

Here we see that the motive of the prescriptions given to the people is not theoretical but real: "Be holy, for I am holy"—that is, I want good for you, and if you do not stay connected to me, you go against this fact.

Thus, the attitude of the Pharisees is abolished at its root. Israel is a kingdom of priests, a holy nation, because it is a people "taken up in" a relationship with God; and to be "priests" in this way is a real fact, not a moral injunction. Israel is a holy people because it belongs to the Lord.

"You shall love the Lord your God with all your heart, and with all your soul, and with all your might. And these words which I command you this day shall be upon your heart; and you shall teach them diligently to your children, and shall talk of them when you sit in your house, and when you walk by the way, and when you lie down, and when you rise" (Deuteronomy 6:5-7).

"The Lord has declared this day concerning you that you are a people for his own possession, as he has promised you, and that you are to keep all his commandments" (Deuteronomy 26:18).

God repeatedly affirms that Israel is his, as of course the rest of the earth also is; but among the peoples, Israel is especially his, a fact established and rooted in history: from which flows our attitude toward concrete life.

In this sense, every hour and every day, every date and every event, has its own importance in the development of our moral life.

The moral life—we repeat—is not a collection of directives and abstract norms with which the will tries to be coherent with grueling effort. If this were the case, we would be strong but alone, and the painful precariousness of this kind of strength is documented in all the greatest spirits of history, outside of the chosen people.

In Christianity, it is something different. Christianity is an engagement with a companionship that gives us strength, that does not exist among any other people, even if all truly human attitudes aspire to this type of moral training. Because outside of the companionship, we enter into the drama of the law, as St. Paul tells us: the more clearly we perceive it, the less we are able to put it into practice.

2.

Who is the person that the Psalms call just or holy?

This person is the one who lives in relationship with God's history, who abandons himself to an historical fact.

Man owes himself to God, not only as his natural origin, but also insofar as man continually receives his meaning in history from God, through the events in which God shows himself. The comparison to the bonds within a natural family and to the love between a man and a woman come closest to this involvement of God with us, a real involvement, from which the necessity of particular behavior springs forth.

> You shall not wrong a stranger or oppress him, for you were strangers in the land of Egypt. You shall not afflict any widow or orphan. If you do afflict them, and they cry out to me, I will surely hear their cry; and my wrath will burn, and I will kill you with the sword, and your wives shall become widows and your children fatherless.
>
> If you lend money to any of my people with you who is poor, you shall not be to him as a creditor, and you shall not exact interest from him. If ever you take your neighbor's garment in pledge, you shall restore it to him before the sun goes down; for that is his only covering, it is his mantle for his body; in what else shall he sleep? And if he cries to me, I will hear, for I am compassionate.
>
> You shall not revile God, nor curse a ruler of your people.
>
> You shall not delay to offer from the fulness of your harvest and from the outflow of your presses.
>
> The first-born of your sons you shall give to me. You shall do likewise with your oxen and with your sheep: seven days it shall be with its dam; on the eighth day you shall give it to me (Exodus 22:21-30).

> If there is among you a poor man, one of your brethren, in any of your towns within your land which the Lord your God gives you, you shall not harden your heart or shut your hand against your poor brother, but you shall open your hand to him, and lend him sufficient for his need, whatever it may be. Take heed lest there be a base thought in your heart, and you say, "The seventh year, the year of release is near," and your eye be hostile to your poor brother, and you give him nothing, and he cry to the Lord against you, and it be sin in you. You shall give to him freely, and your heart shall not be grudging when you give to him; because for this the Lord your God will bless you in all your work and in all that you undertake. For the poor will never cease out of the land; therefore I command you, You shall open wide your hand to your brother, to the needy and to the poor, in the land.
>
> If your brother, a Hebrew man, or a Hebrew woman, is sold to you, he shall serve you six years, and in the seventh year you shall let him go free from you (Deuteronomy 15:7-12).

> You shall not oppress a hired servant who is poor and needy, whether he is one of your brethren or one of the sojourners who are in your land within your towns; you shall give him his hire on the day he earns it, before the sun goes down (for he is poor, and sets his heart upon it); lest he cry against you to the Lord, and it be sin in you.
>
> The fathers shall not be put to death for the children, nor shall the children be put to death for the fathers; every man shall be put to death for his own sin.
>
> You shall not pervert the justice due to the sojourner or to the fatherless, or take a widow's garment in pledge; but you shall remember that you were a slave in Egypt and the Lord your God redeemed you from there; therefore I command you to do this.
>
> When you reap your harvest in your field, and have forgotten a sheaf in the field, you shall not go back to get it; it shall be for the sojourner, the fatherless, and the widow; that the Lord your God may bless you in all the work of your hands. When you beat your olive trees, you shall not go over the boughs again; it shall be for the sojourner, the fatherless, and the widow. When you gather the grapes of your vineyard, you shall not glean it afterward; it shall be for the sojourner, the fatherless, and the widow. You shall remember that you were a slave in the land of Egypt; therefore I command you to do this (Deuteronomy 24:14-22).

There is no difference between this and what St. Paul says in the Letter to the Corinthians: "Do you not know that your body is a temple of the

Holy Spirit within you, which you have from God?" He does not make an analysis of our moral duty but indicates a fact from which a direction and a path of life are born. Any other position tends to make a man his own judge and the creator of a self-sufficient life and therefore an eminent, if desperate, Pharisee.

Man instead finds himself immersed in a fact through which God engages with him, and the necessary attitude becomes obedience—that is, to follow this great companionship.

3.

Not to be faithful to this fact or to forget about it are truly and deeply our responsibility. Sin depends on our freedom: God, in fact, has invited us into his family and let us call him Father.

Infidelity for us does not derive from some outside factor, the "world" of which we are victims, because we have been freed from the world. It derives from our responsibility.

Infidelity comes from our wicked heart. The Bible, in fact, even when it judges idolatry, in reality accuses the Israelites who let themselves be approached by idols, even when they knew how useless those idols were.

God has freed us, and in this freedom consists our justice or our injustice: in accepting or refusing this fact. Man's drama, the temptation of Adam, occurs in *setting ourselves up as judges of this fact.*

Here, then, is the dynamic of sin, the substitution of the criterion established by the fact of God with our own criterion.

The first eleven chapters of Genesis are nothing but the documentation of humanity's affirmation of a criterion that sets itself above the fact of God, because God's command at first seems absurd to man's rationality.

Our human rationality tends only to recognize as rational what we can demonstrate, what is measurable in our immediate experience, whereas even rationality must transcend itself and move toward a fact that exceeds our measure. This attitude is extremely difficult. So often the educated person, when affirming revelation, tends to reduce it to his own cultural schemes without letting himself *be converted* by the mystery that makes itself a *fact* in history.

> Jesus said to them, "Truly, truly, I say to you, the Son can do nothing of his own accord, but only what he sees the Father doing; for whatever he does, that the Son does likewise. For the Father loves

the Son, and shows him all that he himself is doing; and greater works than these will he show him, that you may marvel. For as the Father raises the dead and gives them life, so also the Son gives life to whom he will. The Father judges no one, but has given all judgment to the Son, that all may honor the Son, even as they honor the Father. He who does not honor the Son does not honor the Father who sent him. Truly, truly, I say to you, he who hears my word and believes him who sent me, has eternal life; he does not come into judgment, but has passed from death to life.

"Truly, truly, I say to you, the hour is coming, and now is, when the dead will hear the voice of the Son of God, and those who hear will live. For as the Father has life in himself, so he has granted the Son also to have life in himself, and has given him authority to execute judgment, because he is the Son of man. Do not marvel at this; for the hour is coming when all who are in the tombs will hear his voice and come forth, those who have done good, to the resurrection of life, and those who have done evil, to the resurrection of judgment.

"I can do nothing on my own authority; as I hear, I judge; and my judgment is just, because I seek not my own will but the will of him who sent me. If I bear witness to myself, my testimony is not true; there is another who bears witness to me, and I know that the testimony which he bears to me is true. You sent to John, and he has borne witness to the truth. Not that the testimony which I receive is from man; but I say this that you may be saved. He was a burning and shining lamp, and you were willing to rejoice for a while in his light. But the testimony which I have is greater than that of John; for the works which the Father has granted me to accomplish, these very works which I am doing, bear me witness that the Father has sent me. And the Father who sent me has himself borne witness to me. His voice you have never heard, his form you have never seen; and you do not have his word abiding in you, for you do not believe him whom he has sent. You search the scriptures, because you think that in them you have eternal life; and it is they that bear witness to me; yet you refuse to come to me that you may have life. I do not receive glory from men. But I know that you have not the love of God within you. I have come in my Father's name, and you do not receive me; if another comes in his own name, him you will receive. How can you believe, who receive glory from one another and do not seek the glory that comes from the only God?" (John 5:19-44).

4.

People more readily hear a judgment from other people who speak according to their own criteria, than the judgment of one who speaks in the name of an *other*, of God: this is the truest aspect of humanity's attempt to place itself as "the measure of all things."

Paul knew this well and warned his disciple Timothy:

> I charge you in the presence of God and of Christ Jesus who is to judge the living and the dead, and by his appearing and his kingdom: preach the word, be urgent in season and out of season, convince, rebuke, and exhort, be unfailing in patience and in teaching. For the time is coming when people will not endure sound teaching, but having itching ears they will accumulate for themselves teachers to suit their own likings, and will turn away from listening to the truth and wander into myths. As for you, always be steady, endure suffering, do the work of an evangelist, fulfil your ministry (2 Timothy 4:1-5).

And in the Letter to the Colossians, this warning is further detailed:

> See to it that no one makes a prey of you by philosophy and empty deceit, according to human tradition, according to the elemental spirits of the universe, and not according to Christ.For in him the whole fulness of deity dwells bodily, and you have come to fulness of life in him, who is the head of all rule and authority. In him also you were circumcised with a circumcision made without hands, by putting off the body of flesh in the circumcision of Christ; and you were buried with him in baptism, in which you were also raised with him through faith in the working of God, who raised him from the dead. And you, who were dead in trespasses and the uncircumcision of your flesh, God made alive together with him, having forgiven us all our trespasses, having canceled the bond which stood against us with its legal demands; this he set aside, nailing it to the cross. He disarmed the principalities and powers and made a public example of them, triumphing over them in him.
>
> Therefore let no one pass judgment on you in questions of food and drink or with regard to a festival or a new moon or a sabbath. These are only a shadow of what is to come; but the substance belongs to Christ. Let no one disqualify you, insisting on self-abasement and worship of angels, taking his stand on visions, puffed up without reason by his sensuous mind, and not holding fast to the Head, from whom the whole body, nourished and knit

> together through its joints and ligaments, grows with a growth that is from God.
>
> If with Christ you died to the elemental spirits of the universe, why do you live as if you still belonged to the world? Why do you submit to regulations, "Do not handle, Do not taste, Do not touch" (referring to things which all perish as they are used), according to human precepts and doctrines? These have indeed an appearance of wisdom in promoting rigor of devotion and self-abasement and severity to the body, but they are of no value in checking the indulgence of the flesh (Colossians 2:8-23).

Part of the true dynamic of sin is that it generates *punishment.*

To render the manifestation and the generation of new life through the fact of Christ's death and resurrection impossible, to back away from the fact of Christ, initiates the destruction of our humanity. We are observing this destruction in our epoch and in our existence, where we tend to affirm a reductive logic about humanity, a logic that in the end denies and destroys humanity.

Outside of the fact of Christ, there is no affirmation of humanity but only the sacrifice of humanity to an ideology: this is the power of darkness that dominates the world. We are the ones called to be a light, to speak, and to judge this world, in spite of the sin by which we too are tempted and so often conquered.

The Bible expresses the concept of punishment with the image of a *desert.* The desert: we could define it as the place where life regresses, where life is made vain. Isaiah says:

> O Lord, in distress they sought you,
> they poured out a prayer
> when your chastening was on them.
> Like a woman with child,
> who writhes and cries out in her pangs
> when she is near her time,
> so were we because of you, O Lord;
> we were with child, we writhed,
> but we gave birth only to wind.
> We have won no victories on earth,
> and no one is born to inhabit the world.
> Your dead shall live, their corpses shall rise.
> O dwellers in the dust, awake and sing for joy!
> For your dew is a radiant dew,
> and the earth will give birth to those long dead.

> Come, my people, enter your chambers,
>   and shut your doors behind you;
> hide yourselves for a little while
>   until the wrath is past.
> For the Lord comes out from his place
>   to punish the inhabitants of the earth for their iniquity;
> the earth will disclose the blood shed on it,
>   and will no longer cover its slain (Isaiah 26:16-21).

And again:

> The vision of all this has become for you like the words of a sealed document. If it is given to those who can read, with the command, "Read this," they say, "We cannot, for it is sealed." And if it is given to those who cannot read, saying, "Read this," they say, "We cannot read."
>
> The Lord said:
> Because these people draw near with their mouths
>   and honor me with their lips,
>   while their hearts are far from me,
> and their worship of me is a human commandment learned by rote;
> so I will again do
>   amazing things with this people,
>   shocking and amazing.
> The wisdom of their wise shall perish,
>   and the discernment of the discerning shall be hidden.
> Ha! You who hide a plan too deep for the Lord,
>   whose deeds are in the dark,
>   and who say, "Who sees us? Who knows us?"
> You turn things upside down!
>   Shall the potter be regarded as the clay?
> Shall the thing made say of its maker,
> "He did not make me";
> or the thing formed say of the one who formed it,
> "He has no understanding" (Isaiah 29:11-16).

Desert. We can point out another word that is synonymous and filled with meaning, another word used by the Bible: *solitude*. Because solitude is really the regression of life, which should instead be relationship. Solitude is a vain strength and an empty action.

The emptiness of action lies in this: that you try to do something, and you are alone, you do not generate anything. Solitude. We have seen that the Bible expresses the concept of desert as a regression of life with dramatic accents: "We brought forth wind" and "the inhabitants of the world have not fallen."

This solitude in our moral life, in my opinion, is documented in the indifference that characterizes our attitude in relationships with others.

If our action is not true and leaves us alone, this solitude is evil, and it is this type of solitude that provokes boredom, that makes us feel that our life is useless, and that is reflected in the end by indifference toward people, toward others. This indifference is an emptiness that inevitably finds a form, in the measure that we still have blood in our veins and energy in our bodies, in a natural affectivity that is purely instinctual.

The source of aridity in our relationships with others is in our sin—that is, in our disinterest, distance, our infidelity to the fact of God among us. Christians collaborate in this aridity when they present to the world a Christian morality that is not Christian but only a moralism. This moralism ends up using Christian words in the same way we might take certain ideas from the words of a dead philosopher.

The Christian fact, instead, makes us love humanity, love others in the most authentic sense of the word, precisely because the Christian fact means intimacy, familiarity, with the God who is our destiny.

5.

Another biblical image that indicates the consequence of sin is that of exile: surrendering to foreign powers, becoming slaves.

> Put on the whole armor of God, that you may be able to stand against the wiles of the devil. For we are not contending against flesh and blood, but against the principalities, against the powers, against the world rulers of this present darkness, against the spiritual hosts of wickedness in the heavenly places (Ephesians 6:11-12).

Surrendering to the darkness, to the worldly powers: this is the alienation of our Christian physiognomy, alienation of the new life brought by Christ. It is an error that we can commit even as Christians.

> Then the Lord said to me, Though Moses and Samuel stood before me, yet my heart would not turn toward this people. Send them out of my sight, and let them go! And when they ask you, "Where shall we go?" you shall say to them, Thus says the Lord:

Those who are for pestilence, to pestilence,
   and those who are for the sword, to the sword;
those who are for famine, to famine,
   and those who are for captivity, to captivity.

I will appoint over them four kinds of destroyers, says the Lord: the sword to slay, the dogs to tear, and the birds of the air and the beasts of the earth to devour and destroy. And I will make them a horror to all the kingdoms of the earth because of what Manas'seh the son of Hezeki'ah, king of Judah, did in Jerusalem.

Who will have pity on you, O Jerusalem,
   or who will bemoan you?
Who will turn aside
   to ask about your welfare?
You have rejected me, says the Lord,
   you keep going backward;
so I have stretched out my hand against you and destroyed you;—
   I am weary of relenting.
I have winnowed them with a winnowing fork
   in the gates of the land;
I have bereaved them, I have destroyed my people;
   they did not turn from their ways.
I have made their widows more in number
   than the sand of the seas;
I have brought against the mothers of young men
   a destroyer at noonday;
I have made anguish and terror
   fall upon them suddenly.
She who bore seven has languished;
   she has swooned away;
her sun went down while it was yet day;
   she has been shamed and disgraced.
And the rest of them I will give to the sword
      before their enemies,
says the Lord (Jeremiah 15:1-9).

6.

To take up again the abandoned road, "to take ourselves up again" in a renewed decision, is called *penitence*, or better: *contrition.*

Contrition is the breaking of the heart, where "breaking the heart" means pain at the separation which is the outcome of our rebellion. We must turn toward *another* and recognize him truly. And recognizing the other among us means recognizing the great fact of our history and our life: Jesus Christ. In saying "Jesus Christ," our tendency is to think back two thousand years ago. Instead, we are concerned here with recognizing the fact, the mystery of Jesus Christ, as a presence: the Church. Contrition is the recognition of this fact in which we are caught up.

We are like a child who throws a tantrum at home: throws himself on the ground, fights back against his mother even physically, breaks things, rebels against her. But the mother knows that she is his mother and that he is her child. When the child repents, he recognizes his mother again, and his repentance is precisely this recognition of his mother as mother, not so much an estimation about what he has done.

For the Christian, repentance is recognizing that we belong to a sphere in which the fact gives meaning to our life, and this position, only this position, makes us humble, without presumption and at the same time without desperation. There is no middle way between this humility that breaks forth from a renewed belonging of the heart and the way of the Pharisees who covered over their sin, explaining away their deficiencies and their desperation.

The majority of people experience this desperation. They walk without much energy and without much drama, living like animals and not human beings, according to a mentality in which the good is drowned and moral energy is buried.

God saves me, the word of God, the memory of the fact he established, saves me. When I discover my sinfulness, he rescues me, calling me again and drawing me close again through that context which is the physical sign of his presence in reality. Then, my personal unity and the energy to keep walking are born again.

Conversation on the Sense of Sin

WE COULD SAY, as a counterpoint to the question, "What makes life worth living?" as an antithesis to the religious sense, that man inevitably experiences a confrontation with his fragility: does man have a primordial sense of sin?

First of all, I would not say an antithesis, a counterpoint, but a paradoxical implication.

It is precisely our demand for something that makes life worth living, when it is existentially felt, that makes us sense a disproportion in us just as we are, the perception of a distance that provokes a struggle. This struggle results in more tension than is necessary and fills us with restlessness and worry, with anxiety.

This disproportion makes our human will collide against the obstacle that ultimately leads to a path that goes beyond the impatience generated by our anxiety, that leads to an expectation with which the soul looks for the object of its satisfaction, the fulfillment of its desire. Anxiety, in fact, expands the search for fulfillment in the encounters that make up our human path, and, if not formally, at least practically, these encounters can often be claimed as a substitute for God, that is, as our reason for living.

Thus, man has a primordial sense of sin inasmuch as, sensing in himself the mystery of his need, he perceives the way of facing reality as something other than obedience to this mystery: he does not let the light of this mystery change or determine his actions. Therefore, his own *preoccupation*, his own *measure*, restlessly impose themselves.

What is the connection between the sense of our limits in the broad sense and the awareness of a more precise lack in view of a personal relationship with God, which is how the Christian understands the sense of sin?

The link is something that passes on from a premonition or a confused perception to the moment in which this premonition is illuminated and specified in all its factors. It is the work of revelation.

There are two factors that revelation illuminates.

First of all, our path to destiny follows an order, a design, a weaving together of steps; it is a story thought up and desired by the powerful love of a God who is Father. This clarity comes from the words of the law, the commandments, the precepts of God. There are many Psalms that express this concept. "Oh, how I love your law! It is my meditation all day long" (Psalm 119:97); "the precepts of the Lord are right, rejoicing the heart; the commandment of the Lord is pure, enlightening the eyes" (Psalm 19:8); "I will never forget your precepts; for by them you have given me life" (Psalm 119:93).

The second factor has to do with our responsibility, the capacity we have to recognize the wisdom of something greater than ourselves, the truth that reveals the meaning of our life, the Lord who "knit me together in my mother's womb" (Psalm 139:13) and even possessed me "before I was conceived"; or else the capacity we have of forgetting God, putting him on the margins, substituting him with something set up by us. We have the capacity to exalt the creature in place of God.

The clarity offered by revelation makes us understand this capacity for error, for subversion and corruption, that can happen in individual moments or repeatedly or can even be turned into a more or less explicit theory of life.

What is the significance of the fact that in Christian tradition we speak of original sin?

It is a warning about man's irresolvable incapacity to let himself be determined by his true destiny when left to his own strength, to adhere adequately to the ultimate meaning of his actions, however he understands that meaning: man's inability to obey the truth (see the last scene of *Brand* by Ibsen). As Ovid says in the *Metamorphoses*: *Sed trahit invitum nova voluntas, aliudque cupido mens aliud suadet: video meliora proboque, deteriora sequor*. "Without wanting it, a strange inclination draws me, and passion suggests one thing to me, while the mind suggests another: I see the best, I say 'it is right,' and I do the worst."

The doctrine of original sin makes us aware of the original ambiguity and error in the long run of even our best intentions. Only the mercy of a power that is not in us but that becomes our companion can put us on the right path. Thus, in Exodus 33:15, Moses exclaims: "If your presence will not go with me, do not carry us up from here"; which corresponds to something of which St. Paul was convinced: *Sufficientia nostra a Deo est* (our capacity comes only from God).

A secular mentality feels repugnance toward this image of weakness and structural incoherence: so much so that it cannot explain the desperate impotence that attends every true perception man has about himself.

Yet there is a remnant of sincerity that remains every time we recognize this desperation in ourselves, in others, and especially in the history of the world.

We can easily say that there is no working hypothesis that more clearly demonstrates the existential and historical situation of humanity than the hypothesis of original sin.

This revelation is also a powerful affirmation of the seriousness of human responsibility (our fragility is understood as the outcome of a responsible act by the first man). It even proclaims the organic, profound relationship between every human person, and between every person and that first couple, from which we can say that the deepest unity between us defines the physiognomy of each person.

And for every person, this responsibility leads us to the heart, the essence of life: our heart finds its *answer*, its *correspondence*, in a presence that provokes us, in a substantial companionship that is revealed as our true foundation. Thus the God of Eden who "came down in the cool of the evening," or the God of Sinai, whose face man cannot see, becomes the friendship of Christ, upon whose shoulders we can find the support that allows us to walk in a truly human way. Dionysius the Areopagite exclaims: "Who could ever speak to us of the love that Christ has for man, overflowing with peace?"

The Bible recounts that Cain, after killing Abel, runs away. What does this image suggest if we apply it to the common modern mentality toward feelings of guilt?

The value of freedom has its foundation only in the relationship we have with the infinite, in the existence in us of something that does not derive totally from the biological inheritance from our parents or of a particular race. Freedom takes its value from the fact that there exists something in us that implies a direct relationship with God—or, as the catechism of Pius X says, that the body is made from the parents but "the soul is infused directly by God." In the contemporary mentality, the confusion and negation of this relationship with God, which is constitutive of the heart, totally blocks the value of freedom, its existential vigor, that is, eclipses an understanding of freedom as responsibility. The awkwardness of our own incoherence, of the disproportion and of the real corruption present in our action, not only tries to censure itself in forgetfulness, in distraction, or in a violent repression—as in every age—but tries to resolve it peacefully or unburden itself by attributing all of its moral disproportion to some determined mechanism, however they conceive of these mechanisms.

The dominant trends of modern psychology try to make the removal of human responsibility, and therefore of human dignity, the common mentality.

A common opinion holds that Christianity, more often than not in the way it is transmitted, has weighed down on man's conscience in a distorting manner, has laid on man an oppressive boulder of guilt and anguish about sin. To what can we attribute this?

I think that the theoretical *specification* of the relationship between us and our destiny in God, if it is not affirmed and faithfully followed in the unity of the event of Christ and of his mysterious body which is the Church, tends to see these factors according to the measure of our natural experience, full of terror in front of an unknown destiny. Therefore, we easily fall prey to an impatient anxiety toward ourselves, which is then turned toward others, with no way of escape in front of our own fragility. We are then stuck in the maze of our own image of justice, a rigid measure that leads us to be intolerant and closed-off. "In order not to be locked up in our feelings, we lock ourselves up in the limits of any sort of justice!" warns Baldwin of Canterbury. Here is the horrible phenomenon in Christianity of moralism: a God made to humanity's measure is a monster who crushes us, and this word is not creative or renewing, corrective, "redemptive," but a judgment that *defines* humanity, that God *takes out* on sinful humanity.

In Christianity, instead, "the truth will set you free," as St. John says. The first truth is the recognition of our own evil limits, of our responsibility for our own incoherence. In front of God who has "no pleasure in the death of the wicked, but that the wicked turn from his way and live," this recognition is the beginning of a liberating breath and makes a humble abandonment, a hope full of joy, possible for the creature. The Christian then reaches a place where it is possible to hope against all hope, in the words of St. Paul.

What is the positive meaning of sin in the history of salvation?

Sin in the story of salvation has a positive sense in two ways.

First of all, sin is the experience in which we verify our own ineptitude and weakness and therefore our incapacity to be ourselves. We sense our nothingness. Jesus says in the Gospel: "Without me you can do nothing." From the metaphysical point of view, this is literally true. And we should be able to intuit it with a simple reflection on our contingency: yesterday I did not exist, and tomorrow I will no longer be here.

We can easily be deceived about this existential consistency, this gift of the creating Word. We interpret it, in fact, as an autonomous consistency, as a limit we put on God's lordship, and therefore a protest against the intrusive, totalizing presence of God. Yet God permits sin, which becomes for us an experience of evil and thus of our incapacity to be true, to be integrally ourselves. Sin becomes the unequivocal verification of our ultimate inconsistency.

A second pedagogical value is inherent in the first. In the naked form of humanity's original nature, which is hunger and thirst for the infinite, for the fulfillment of the self, this humiliating impossibility of walking on our own disposes us to look for something that would permit us to overcome our waywardness. It pushes us to search for what can heal us of this mortal wound. The sense of sin is thus an education in waiting for Christ; it builds in us an understanding of the supreme advantage of God's offer of help; it disposes us to a newness for which we long. It is as if the initiative of God were made unconsciously acceptable and familiar to us. Christ arrives as the long-awaited friend.

Ultimately, I believe that the positive sense of sin in the history of salvation consists in this: the Word became flesh to redeem us from sin. The paradox pointed out by St. Augustine is undeniably evident: "O felix culpa."

The word forgiveness has been emptied of its meaning in the language of our society today. Normally, a nuance of weakness is added to it, almost as if forgiveness is owed to a person who is not able to react differently because of the fault by which he is weighed down. Why? What is the meaning of forgiveness in Christianity?

The word forgiveness has been emptied of its meaning in our daily usage, it has become only an indicator of humanity's weakness, because, for today's society, the value of our humanity, our dignity, is not understood. Humanity's value no longer comes from channeling all of its energies toward the end of life, and therefore it no longer comes from its ability to comprehend a meaning, a design, the totality of factors in play; but rather, it comes from affirming itself, a self that is identified by the feeling that most predominates in the moment. Therefore, our value comes from a partiality that is violently affirmed; all that is left is a reaction (opinion, interest, instinct), and this is incapable of pursuing the ideal.

Christian forgiveness is an imitation of the luminous and calm power with which the Father rebuilds the destiny of his creatures, surprising them and helping them discover their permanent and essential desire for good, a desire which remains even after all the disasters that result from our presumptuous and impatient self-affirmation. Thus, forgiveness is God's omnipotence which starts to build again on the last residual traces of freedom in us: "Forgive them, Father, for they know not what they do," as Jesus will say on the cross.

If an enemy who hates me, while he is about to strike me to death, would only realize what it means for me to say to him, "I forgive you." If he were intelligent, he would be overcome with anger, because at the same time he is killing me, he cannot stop me from embracing him. And his animosity is a reaction to, and paradoxically dependent on, my awareness and affirmation of the ultimate meaning of everything.

Sin and forgiveness of sin are linked in Christian tradition by the Sacrament of Confession. Is there a wisdom in this gesture instituted by the Church?

And what wisdom! Without the ability to compare ourselves with something that is not us—without this objective confrontation—the recognition of our error is less convincing. It cannot be a true repentance if it does not include this turning to something outside of ourselves, this acknowledgement in front of others and the world. While the sacrament takes place with the highest discretion, the priest, to whom we confess our evil, still represents the presence of the whole ecclesial community.

Without the sign of this objectivity, even forgiveness fluctuates in uncertainty, is linked to the volubility of our own state of soul, and our heart bounces between the dangers of presumption and sentimental illusion on one side and of discouragement and desperation on the other. Both of these dangers are preludes to cynicism. In any case, forgiveness does not bring true peace if it does not echo the judgment of that human community which is the sign of God.

Structurally, we are made in such a way that this objectivity, if it is not anchored in the work of Christ, the Church, in the visible communion of the Church, will be sought in society and determined by the common mentality. Even criminal actions, from the point of view of our God-given nature, leave the conscience anxious at first, but, when a human tribunal declares a man free of blame, this anxiety subsides in the illusion of one's own justice.

But to accept the forgiveness that is continually offered us by God, because we continually sin, implies a radical change in front of the mentality that we absorb today. It would, in fact, be understandable to mess up and be pardoned once, twice, three times, but then someone would say: "You must have a minimum of coherence; it is too easy just to rely on God's pardon." What does Christianity say to this idea?

Because of our fragility, we are incapable of fulfilling ourselves, which means, in the long run, that we are not capable of traveling our path without grave contradictions in ourselves. "Children, how hard it is to enter the kingdom of God!"; "Then who can be saved?"; "With men it is impossible, but not with God; for all things are possible with God" (cf. Mark 10:17-27).

The only correct posture for us is to cry to God from within the reality of our own potential and actual sin, to request forgiveness—so that the power of God may accomplish an otherwise impossible change.

This change is always a miracle of God, a grace that is always given when we request it in the right way (cf. Luke 11:1-10). With this request, in fact, there always comes a change in the self, yet the way this change is fulfilled and the time of its fulfillment are in the hands of God.

The only requirement is that this cry must be existentially true and sincere; to accept the discomfort of this truth is the first step toward change.

How do we Christians respond to the unbearableness that easily comes over us when, due to the clamor of our weakness, we have to look this misery in the face?

This is a great occasion for love, a great occasion for a loving affirmation.

The truth about our humanity cannot be reduced to the observation of its misery but to the wondrous and exalting announcement that this misery is loved. This loving, strong, and faithful presence, more than the fickle and vulnerable fragility that is the substance of humanity when left to itself, is our true richness. And we are not saying that the evidence of our own misery is always the point of departure, the initial discovery; because it is actually within the brilliance of the announcement of a presence that we are able to discover our own nakedness, our own ineptitude, our own poverty.

Therefore, the presence of another is the consistency—the certainty and hope—of humanity: to accept this, to affirm this, is to live existence as love. To love is to affirm that another is the essence of my life and that my life is found in the affirmation of another. "You are me." "It is no longer I who live, but Christ who lives in me" (Galatians 2:20).

The response of Christianity to this intolerance toward ourselves is a humility that becomes love; it is the recognition of our own misery (*humus* = earth) that opens itself to the rich presence of another and recognizes him, rejoices in him, in his love.

The liturgy of the Church has us say during every Mass: "You who take away the sins of the world, have mercy on us." What does this phrase mean? How can the sins of the world be taken away?

This question sums up our whole understanding of salvation. Christ died to free us from our evil. The infinite value of the victim in this mysterious economy makes up for humanity's untold deficiencies in two ways.

The first is implied in the cry of Christ on the cross: "Father, forgive them, for they know not what they do." This is a comprehensive love that surpasses anything we could imagine and brings about our redemption. The cry on the cross relies on that trace, however infinitesimal, of our ignorance and covers the gap that always exists between human wickedness and the great fact of God.

The second is that in the decay of the human heart, from within our human weakness, a cry arises for this humanly impossible liberation, a liberation that is only possible for God: Lord, have mercy on me.

Conclusion

The Church as the Place of Morality

1. Christian Morality: Adhesion, Not Measure

THE MORAL PERSON is the one who lives the original attitude with which the Creator shaped her; this means that, in whatever way she is conscious of it, she adheres to and maintains it, desires it. The original attitude in which we were created is a force with a particular direction and a precise end, a tension toward the mystery itself who placed it there, a stretching out toward the infinite God; *Fecisti nos ad te, Domine, et irrequietum est cor nostrum donec requiescat in te:* "You have made us for yourself, O Lord, and our heart is restless until it rests in you" (St. Augustine).

The essence of morality lies in living the moment within this tension, in facing, more or less consciously and explicitly, every action from within this tension.

It is in this sense that an authentic morality cuts through our personal error and sin. This authentic morality remains faithful to itself by judging the fact that we succumb to weakness, rebellion, or incoherence. It judges how the act in which we express ourselves is capable of subverting the direction of that original attitude. And precisely in this *judgment*, true affection is able to prevail—that is, the energy to adhere to the end toward which our natural dynamism is destined.

Our existential condition is such that, in this continual journey, the moral path draws closer and closer to its horizon. In the continual reaffirmation of the ultimate value, in spite of all our failure and violence, the human person grows in affection for this value by always adhering to it. This existential condition affirms being even while feeling contrition within its relationships, constructs its human face even while knowing its need for conversion.

Our human face is built up as an amazed affection for itself; it is amazed because we are always able to find it again within the dust and ruins. It is a gift, an intangible grace, the sign of a presence that constitutes us. At the same time, it is an affection full of energy, because by nature the search for this human face is a movement of adherence to the one who is our intrinsic destination, the unknown that we must recognize, the unlimited that we must embrace, the perfection that we must imitate. "Be perfect as your heavenly Father is perfect": Christian morality is not a measure to live up to; it is the adhesion to a presence, to the Being who is the original mystery that constitutes the human creature.

2. The Emergence of an Objective Reference

We must note that all this understanding of adherence does not lay the foundation for a situational ethic, understood as an ethical directive determined by the "moment," that is, by the reaction that the unrepeatable circumstances generate within this tension. In fact, the mystery of God reveals a path into which the creature's affection must channel itself. An objectivity emerges that goes beyond the emotion of our human reaction.

This objectivity has to do with *the nature of things*, that inevitable point of reference, and thus with the unity of the divine design that is the foundation for the unity of created things among themselves.

This movement toward God, which is morality, can never, at least ultimately, circumvent or contradict this objective human face.

3. Man, on the Threshold of the Mystery, "Pretends" to Be God

On the other hand, abandoned to ourselves, we are only able to maintain the right path with difficulty. We cannot stand up straight on that dizzying threshold where the mystery is recognized as mystery and is obeyed in the undeniable diversity—and at the same time coherence—of the things that continually emerge from his infinite creativity.

We cannot stand for long on that great threshold; we get easily distracted or fall into our dreams about the mystery. We make up a God in our own image and likeness, invent and manipulate the meaning of things according to the demands of our own projects.

The morality of ideology tends to make up its own God (thus destroying the ultimate function of contrition) in order to build a life according to its own measure. Moralism turns into the prison of freedom.

But even when our projects and expectations are purely formulated, we inevitably experience the humiliation of incoherence.

"Wretched man that I am! Who will deliver me from this body of death?"

4. The Church: A Merciful Presence

"Who"—we already know it.

"Who will separate us from the love of Christ?"

Obedience to Christ forces us to acknowledge where the "work of God" enters our lives and where we can discover an objective rule of life, a rock on which we can build, an incorruptible life.

The Church is the place where the presence of Christ becomes mercy for us; the longed-for terminus of the aspiration that constitutes us becomes the objective place where I can follow. The unique and enigmatic design, which everything and every moment hint at, becomes a new reality on the earth, in history, a sign—because it is the beginning—of the total victory of Christ.The true face of things, the inherent goal that gives them consistency, is clearly defined here: the word of Christ, protected and proclaimed by the Church, gives a response to our human dreams. At the same time, the world around us tends to cover over this truth by scaring us with monstrous figures or deceiving us with false certainties and promises. The word of God corrects those deviations which anxiety, impatience, self-love, and the thirst for power tend to force upon us, whether in the misery of the individual or the presumption of the collective.

The radicality of this light, with which the word of God introduces the abiding significance of things, allows us to face our destiny with solid tools by which we know how and where to put our energies. The articulation of things according to human manipulation thus acquires the possibility of a clarity which gives greater value to things and makes the use of our time more intense. This great gift involves all the freedom of our thought, of our imagination, of our decisions and our practices.

The Church is the place where we receive this gift of clarity, of security, and of "yielding" in the relationship between man, things, and time.

5. The Games of Relativism and Skepticism

Outside of the Church, whether we are aware of it or not, humanity gropes around in an attempt to narrow in on the true meaning of things and to define their final outcome, the efficacy of their presence, the order of relations.

It is difficult outside of the Church to avoid the skepticism and relativism that creep into this search, not only where the search becomes uncertain, but even where it remains presumptuous.

We must also observe how the relativistic attitude cannot avoid the law whereby everything we make can only be certain by building itself on a security; otherwise, it is a castle made of sand whose destruction looms threateningly over us even as we try to put stone on stone. Therefore, the relativist, in his practical life and in the urgency of his projects, absolutizes the point of view that interests him, and in his relationships with others tends to impose something on them and unconsciously on himself.

Thus, an abnormal instrumentalization of the self, of others, and of things do not derive only from an anxious restlessness but more directly and forcefully from the restlessness of a will to power that seeks security and consistency in success.

It is in the holiness of the Church that this complex game is unmasked, fought, and overcome. The ultimate meaning is a presence; the clearness of the Church's vision searches within the ambiguity of mere appearances and discovers the real usefulness of things; in particular, time exorcises the hostility of which death and corruption are the supreme signs: the work of this presence in the world is difficult, but peaceful. The work of life becomes patience.

6. *Living Memory: The Essence of Morality*

We must take up another point. The certainty that time creates an order, and thus is ultimately favorable, does not come from our own analysis, and therefore it is not based on the energy of our own will forcing reality to fit our own perspective: this would lead to the absence of peace.

Our certainty is founded on a presence. The favor of this presence makes the outcome of our efforts in time secure.

But this is not just an event that happens outside the effort of our own thought and freedom. Like a son walking beside his father, like a disciple in front of the true master, like a friend close by his friend, we are able to see *from within this relationship* and how it works with an energy that is continually *given by that relationship*.

It is as if the first object of our attention is this presence—not a *duty* to accomplish something. It is as if the first object of our affection is this presence—not a reality to possess. It is as if the first place that draws our energy is this presence—not our own ethical strength. The clarity of a moral judgment, the affective inclination toward justice, the strength of will—all this matures as a consequence: in fact, the relationship with that presence attracts and raises up the whole person.

Morality in the Church is first of all an event: the recognition of that presence and *being* with him. *To live memory*—this is the morality of Christian holiness.

7. Memory Anchored in a Sign

Memory is anchored in a sign. And familiarity with this sign, which we grasp with the eyes of a child and maintain in poverty of heart, guarantees vigilance. We are vigilant that the image we have of ourselves conform itself to reality, a reality which, while hidden, is made clear in its most existentially significant traits and which works through the objective structure of a sign. "And whoever has this hope purifies himself as he is pure."

For *homo viator*, this sign-memory (memorial), the inexhaustible source of this hope, and thus of the mobilization of freedom, is the Eucharist. The profound relationship of Christian life with this sacrament invests that life with the fervor for ethics. Our Christian life depends on the sacrament, and from it draws freshness for a renewed moral engagement (cf. 1 Corinthians 10:14-22). The sacrament offers a decisive context for the right and fitting attitude (cf. 1 Corinthians 11:18-24).

But the Eucharistic sign expands itself and clarifies itself in an even bigger sign, the Church, the truest sign of Christ's presence, "the fulness of him who fills all in all" (Ephesians 1:23).

This "body, joined and knit together by every joint with which it is supplied, when each part is working properly, makes bodily growth and upbuilds itself in love" (Ephesians 4:16); this body is thus the place where morality breaks forth and finds nourishment: "building itself up in love."

The aim of the Church's education to Christian morality is this: to raise up the self-awareness of the person as one who belongs totally to the unity of the bond begun in Baptism (cf. Galatians 3:26-29), a unity guarded and developed by an authority (cf. Ephesians 2:19-21), and to motivate the expression of this awareness in service to the community.

The interaction of the self and the community—in so far as this mystery is recognized, loved, and embraced—makes a new measure and sensibility penetrate our personality, as by an osmotic pressure. This changed life (*metanoia*) makes a new *delectatio victrix* (conquering delight) possible, makes the building up of virtue easier. This new joy—complete joy (cf. 1 John 1:4)—creates a hope that remains "against all hope."

The Church repeats the words of St. Thomas: *O memoriale mortis Domini . . . praesta meae menti de te vivere, et te illi semper dulce sapere* ("O memorial of our Lord's death . . . Grant my soul to live on you, and always to savor your sweetness").

The whole density of an authentic Christian moral life leads back to these factors.

This book was set in Adobe Caslon Pro, designed by Carol Twombly and released in 1990. The typeface is named after the British typefounder William Caslon (1692–1766) and grew out of Twombly's study of Caslon's specimen sheets produced between 1734 and 1770. Though Caslon began his career making "exotic" typefaces—Hebrew, Arabic, and Coptic—his Roman typeface became the standard for text printed in English for most of the eighteenth century, including the Declaration of Independence.

This book was designed by Shannon Carter, Ian Creeger, and Gregory Wolfe. It was published in hardcover, paperback, and electronic formats by Slant Books, Seattle, Washington.

Cover art: *Fayum Mummy Portrait*, Fayum oasis, Egypt, AD 54-68, British Museum.

www.ingramcontent.com/pod-product-compliance
Lightning Source LLC
LaVergne TN
LVHW091147080826
845145LV00008B/2290

* 9 7 8 1 6 3 9 8 2 1 9 0 7 *